D1468476

SELF–WEALTH™

Creating Prosperity, Serenity,
and Balance in Your Life

Mark Yarnell
Valerie Bates
John Radford

Other Books by Mark Yarnell:

Power Multi-Level Marketing

Power Speaking

Your First Year in Network Marketing

Self-Wealth™

Creating Prosperity, Serenity, and Balance in Your Life

Mark Yarnell
Valerie Bates
John Radford

Paper Chase Press
New Orleans, LA

SELF-WEALTH™:

Creating Prosperity, Serenity, and Balance in your Life

Copyright ©1999
Mark Yarnell, Valerie Bates, John Radford

ISBN: 1-879706-74-1
LC: 98-068589

Cover Design:
Multifresh.com, Portland, OR

Paper Chase Press books may be purchased for educational, business or sales promotional use. For information, please write: Special Markets Department, Paper Chase Press, 5721 Magazine Street, Suite 152, New Orleans, LA 70115.

FIRST EDITION
Printed in the United States

121141

DEDICATION

We dedicate this book to those who:

Assume the challenge of leaving the world a better place

Dare to truly love

And have taught us the most about Self-Wealth...

Our families—Moms and Dads, Lorraine, Hannah-Rose, Amy,

Christine, and Eric.

ACKNOWLEDGEMENTS

We thank:

Dr. Albert Bandura whose book *Self-Efficacy* and countless years of scholastic and psychological research inspired us to write this book.

Our friends who shared their stories.

Bill Burkett, our editor, who so gamely took on the challenge of integrating the work of three writers and undauntingly challenged us to achieve greater clarity.

Werner Riefling, publisher of Paper Chase Press, whose professionalism has been unwaivering throughout this project.

CONTENTS

Introduction

It has been stated quite succinctly that those who live with little contentedly, posses everything. But this philosophy has not appealed to a vast number of people, who suspected that it might be just a rationalization to justify an inability to seize an opportunity and exert the energy necessary to achieve material wealth.

"Think and Grow Rich" was the battle cry of millions as the twentieth century wound to a close. It became quite in vogue to assert that riches and fame were there to be accumulated for all who could but harness the remarkable power of reflective, positive contemplation, instead of hard, dedicated work. This movement was fuelled by the clear evidence that hard, dedicated work, in and of itself, often failed to provide the expected rewards.

Entire schools of thought emerged around charismatic leaders who taught the concept of abundance without effort. One individual abandoned all worldly responsibilities, including a family and mortgage, to write back-to-back bestsellers, one about a bird who dared to undergo the metamorphosis from seagull to eagle, then a love story about his new-found romance. Those and countless other "positive thinking" books advocated wealth without effort, and love without responsibilities. But expecting a miracle and praying for unexpected income didn't work for most, and millions became cynical and disillusioned.

The 1980s were known as the "greed" decade. Countless individuals became victims of carnival barkers and brokers who thought nothing of amassing personal millions at the expense of pensioners. Situation ethics ruled the day and everyone believed wealth was doable...wealth meaning money. Countless innocents with no inherent skills, honest mentor, or step-by-step practical systems began to enter the investment and no-money-down arenas, armed merely with pop-psychology principles of positive thought.

There were plenty of self-appointed prosperity gurus to lead them toward what one popular ad promised was: "A Lazy Man's Way to Riches." The last part of the century became a financial feeding frenzy for a handful of articulate sales types, and a fiscal disaster for many gullible citizens.

While thinking about positive outcomes was certainly an improvement over the "lives of quiet desperation" described by one of our earliest American philosophers, Henry David Thoreau, positive thinking alone is not the route to lasting fulfillment and serenity.

Stress-related diseases increased at an alarming rate, especially among career women. Child abuse skyrocketed, as did alcoholism and drug addiction. Prison populations quadrupled between 1960 and 1980 and doubled again in the next decade.

Median incomes rose slowly, but social problems grew exponentially. The end of the 1990s was so paradoxical that a U.S. President had to fight impeachment proceedings while enjoying a 72 percent approval rating from the entire American population.

Something just didn't seem to feel right.

Computers are changing our world, but productivity in many workforces fell below levels of the 1950s as employees were forced to spend more time in computer training to keep pace with technological advances. Millions of mid-level managers were laid off as large and small companies began to look at short-term profit pictures, not the needs of their employees' families. Downsizing outstripped productivity as a profit enhancer, and those companies willing to cut management teams to the bone became the darlings of Wall Street.

Displaced, unemployed, formerly successful six-figure executives formed clubs and self-help groups to counsel one another and practice resume writing. People weren't happy, and it wasn't just the traditional have-nots who were disillusioned. The American dream had become a nightmare for all strata of society. Success and failure to succeed seemed to be equally hollow concepts.

We believe there were three reasons for the mass disillusionment, and we are going to offer three answers to them.

First, the concept of wealth was ill-defined. We intend to redefine wealth in this book to include those things which produce lasting human fulfillment. We fervently believe that material acquisitions alone produce no meaningful basis for sustained serenity. We believe that the process of greedily seeking worldly treasures is an exercise in futility that leads to bigotry, wars, hatred and violence. When we achieved real material wealth, we soon recognized the absurdity of conspicuous consumption.

Second, we want to address the fallacious assumptions which arise from erroneous thinking. What we think others believe about us, and what we think about ourselves can serve to undermine our happiness. Or we can change our thoughts to enhance our happiness. There *is* that germ of truth in all the positive-thinking approaches.

But merely trying to be "positive" isn't enough. We need tools and an action plan to redesign our previously ineffective thoughts and practices. And that's what we're offering you in this book. Our past reactions to life's circumstances have colored our thinking, often to our detriment. There are specific ways to rearrange our thoughts to enhance our lives, and there has been abundant research to prove these methods work. We're going to share some of those methods for correcting erroneous thinking with you.

Finally, we will to give you specific information on how to design a step-by-step game plan for redefining your Self-Wealth, rearranging your thinking into effective patterns, and then *taking action* to bring new results into your reality.

We don't pretend to offer definitive solutions to all, or even most, problems we all face. We aren't blessed with the gift of prophecy. None of us alive today can truly look into the new millenium and predict the challenges we will face.

But the three of us have accumulated quite a bit of information which suggests that whatever those challenges are, your best preparation for them begins right now, today, and it begins in your own thoughts. We hope that our treatment of this subject matter of Self-Wealth will positively influence you in the months ahead, and help you become more self-confident as you face the new millenium.

For ease of reading and clarity purposes we have written this book in the first person singular; however, each writer has contributed one-third of the chapters in this collaborative work.

We've thoroughly enjoyed the process of writing this book. That enjoyment, as you will soon see, is the basis of true Self-Wealth. The best thinkers in history have asserted that true Self-Wealth is founded in joy. Self-Wealth is a process not a destination. Cervantes, author of *Don Quixote,* wrote "the journey is better than the inn."

True human satisfaction comes through the process of owning your own thoughts, selecting your life's endeavors, and moving forward confidently in the direction of your dreams. A dream we three have shared is now in your hands. The creation of this book, and getting it to you, is reward enough for our efforts.

Our finest reward, however, will be if you take the lessons from this little book and apply them with passion to your own life, and your own lifelong quest for Self-Wealth.   Let's begin!

CHAPTER 1

A Goal Bigger Than Yourself:

The Foundation of Self-Wealth

"The measure of life is not its duration, but its donation."

Peter Marshall

In April 1986 I found myself financially, emotionally and spiritually bankrupt in Austin, Texas. The bank was repossessing my car, the savings and loan was foreclosing on my home, my best friend had embezzled my only assets, and on top of it all, I was drinking heavily. Recently divorced, my emotions were raw and my nerves were shot. As a college dropout with no viable track record or significant business experience, I had no prospects for immediate employment.

With my back against the wall, I decided to shift my attention away from myself and boldly focus on someone worse off than me. It was a wildly unorthodox move, but I was out of orthodox ones. I decided to create a goal bigger than myself.

At the time, the Austin City Council was struggling with an overwhelming homeless problem. A gentleman from Houston was lobbying them to create a free drug and alcohol center for street people. His reasoning was that nearly 80 percent of all homeless people had a drug or alcohol problem. The local government had rejected his proposal based on the overwhelming costs associated with such a project. I decided to create the funding myself, and in the process, get sober. Ambitious? You bet! But the objective seemed so worthwhile that I quit drinking and wrote out my goal to create the revenue necessary to bring the project to life.

No sooner had the ink dried on my goal sheet than a friend called me with an entrepreneurial venture which offered the possibility of making a lot of money. It would require very hard work, but virtually no financial investment. That part fit: I had no finances to invest!

I knew very little about business, but I managed to find a mentor who had been extremely successful in that particular kind of endeavor. He agreed to coach me, and I went to work. One year later I was earning over $30,000 a month, was clean and sober, involved in a meaningful personal relationship, and had provided a significant amount of money for the free treatment center.

A decade later I had millions in assets, was writing for *Success* magazine, and had become the proud recipient of Philanthropist of the Year Award from the *Washington* (D.C.) *Times*.

Overnight Success

It took me years of hard work to become an overnight success. I had many challenges and setbacks, but perseverance and resilience finally paid off. The fact is Self-Wealth is hard work. Sometimes success seems best defined by Thomas Edison, who wrote: "success is moving from failure to failure gracefully."

There are always ups and downs, and unpredictable life circumstances. Perseverance and resiliency will always triumph over adversity and failure eventually. Applying all of the principles in this book will work for you as they did for me. One thing you will discover is that the only certainty is change.

Real joy and serenity will not be found by arriving in a comfort zone of effortless bliss. Serenity will come when you are confident that you can reach such a zone whenever you choose.

My material wealth can be taken away in its entirety. I know what it is like to have a great deal of material wealth and then lose it for various reasons. But I don't let the loss of material wealth trouble me too much. Remember, change is the only constant. I simply begin accumulating more. The mental state of the true Self-Wealth achiever is perhaps best embodied by *Mad* magazine character Alfred E. Neumann: "What, me worry?"

Bouncing Back Again, and Again

A truly inspiring story of a friend and colleague of mine, Gary Haiser, is a prime example of perseverance and resilience. Here is Gary's story:

Self-Wealth

"Life for me has been a series of mental, physical, and financial ups and downs beginning at an early age. At thirteen, I thought I was on top of the world. I grew up in the mid-west, was the oldest of four children and had a tremendous family life. We lived in a nice home in a middle class neighborhood, were enrolled in the best public school system in the state, had lots of friends and loving, successful parents... What more could a kid ask for?

"Then, my world changed dramatically and suddenly. It was Christmas Eve and we had just kissed our folks goodnight and went to bed all excited about the holiday ahead. We were suddenly awakened that night to the screams of our mother, who was trying desperately to wake Dad up. He had fallen asleep on the couch and slipped into a coma. He was just 38 years old. Dad died of a rare blood disease that night and I grew up quickly afterwards. Playing baseball with Dad cheering me on from the sidelines, and all the other father-son events was suddenly erased from my life.

"That was the first, and most traumatic, life-altering event that forced me to evaluate my options in life. I had to go on. I had to rise above the pain and anger of the tremendous loss I felt. He was a great father, friend and my mentor. Something he taught me and said often helped pull me through. He told me over and over again, 'Gary, you can do anything in life you set your mind to. Never let anyone else's opinion stop you from trying.'

"That advice, plus the strength and courage of my mother who raised us on her own, set the stage for my rediscovery and comeback after several other set-backs in my life.

"Following in the footsteps of my father, I became a building contractor in my early 20's with a childhood buddy who also grew up in a family of contractors. Our business was booming in the early 70's and the local paper featured us as one of the most successful young building companies in the area. Then, just as we were about to become the largest home-improvement contractor in our state, the 1974 recession hit. It wiped us out. The banks would no longer loan us money for expansion. Our jobs began to dry up. Our accounts payable grew and grew and our cash flow dwindled to the point where we couldn't pay our help...or ourselves. It was over. I lost two homes, a business and my marriage came to an end all at the same time.

"Once again, I had to draw upon the strength and courage my parents instilled in me at an early age. Circumstances beyond our control had forced us out of business. We had a choice. Give up and accept a life of mediocrity or find another way to succeed. I chose success. Failure and mediocrity were not options.

"I read books, listened to positive audio tapes every day and told myself daily that I was a winner. I was going to the top of whatever I decided to do. I would not be denied the success I dreamed about!

"Were there more business failures for me? You bet there were...lots more. Too many to talk about here. But the best part of failing is the knowledge and experience you gain from it. You become stronger and wiser. Success becomes easier for you, especially if you have a burning desire to succeed and confidence in yourself.

"My life is really working today. I am married to the most fantastic woman alive. We have three grown children who are all successful, responsible adults. We have thirteen beautiful grandchildren and live a life that most people would give their left arm for. Yes, we have had many business failures, yet we have managed to gross millions of dollars in recent years working right out of our home in Florida.

"What are we up to now? We're building another business of course! Chances are, we'll make another fortune with it because we have learned one of the most valuable lessons in life along the way. Success is simply a journey, not a destination. Making a difference in other people's lives, having faith in your dreams and a reason to get up in the morning is the answer to a lot of life's challenges. We also continue to live by my late father's words...'You can do anything in life you set your mind to. And never let other people's opinions keep you from trying.'"

Meaningful Achievements Are What You Make Them

Meaningful achievements obviously require tenacity and perseverance. I am convinced that the underlying basis for my success to overcome life's challenges stemmed from the simple decision to shift my life's focus from personal problems to a goal bigger than myself.

This may seem a bit "airy-fairy" to you pragmatic readers. But there is no greater motivation than a personal crusade that elevates your thinking beyond self-centered concerns and focuses on a grander vision. Undoubtedly that's what sent Albert Schweitzer to darkest Africa to finish his remarkable career among illiterate natives. It drove Mother Theresa to the hell-hole of Calcutta to found hospitals for lepers. It was the catalyst that inspired Ghandi to free an entire nation that became the largest democracy in the world.

You may think that such a vision necessitates a lifetime vow of personal financial poverty. That is not necessarily true. You make a choice to be poor. Consider the words of one of Ghandi's public relations people a week after Ghandi's death: "You have no idea how much it cost us to keep him in poverty." Ghandi chose personal poverty—but he still had lots of overhead. You can focus on and achieve significant altruistic goals—and nothing is more satisfying than helping others—and still enjoy personal financial wealth. It's your choice.

Material Wealth is Good

It is important for Self-Wealth aspirants to understand that it's morally and spiritually good to have wealth. Early in the Fourth century some pious Catholic leaders decided to take vows of poverty and live in caves. They were known as monks and were highly respected as moral people, thus poverty became a virtue. Of course, they also flogged themselves daily to prove their worth through suffering, a practice ignored today, and equally absurd.

As my good friend Dr. Roy Blizzard, author of the scholarly book *Understanding the Difficult Words of Jesus*, points out, even young Jesus never taught that money was bad. The only officer he appointed among his twelve disciples was a treasurer. He watched to see who put what in the offering plates. He once even chided a wealthy man who tithed only half his assets. Jesus rode everywhere on a donkey while followers fanned Him with palm leaves and everybody else walked. When he died, his seamless robe was of such value that the Roman soldiers created a mini-lottery to draw for it.

Hindus, Buddhists, Muslims, Orthodox Jews and Christians all recognize the value of money as long as we avoid attachments to worldly affluence. For it is in the misappropriated love of wealth that most people find themselves leading shallow lives. Properly understood, money becomes the greatest ally of those committed to purposeful lives.

Serenity, Balance & Fulfillment

Serenity, balance and fulfillment are the name of the game before you can achieve true Self-Wealth. You can have all three, independent of or in addition to material wealth, personal prestige and worldly power. In my own case, creating and achieving a goal bigger than myself did indeed encompass material wealth, personal prestige, and a certain amount of power. But I learned that the most important aspect of my achievement was serenity, balance and the sense of fulfillment I experienced. The money is important, but it is not enough.

The important lesson here is that material acquisition and gratifying your ego through power and prestige are not satisfying in and of themselves. I believe you must freely give of yourself and your money before you truly achieve a sense of fulfillment in life. Just acquiring material wealth for your own gratification, or finding ways to gratify your ego, will leave you empty. Such an attempt at gratification becomes a hole that can never be filled. Trust me on this, although I'm certain some cynical readers are probably thinking: "Yeah, sure. Just give me a few million dollars and I'll have all the serenity, balance and fulfillment I need."

Many people who have acquired a great deal of wealth have been through the usual song and dance: they purchased all the customary toys (the cars, planes, boats, etc.), enjoyed world travel, experienced applause and adulation in business and social circles, and so on. But you soon come to realize that acquiring a bigger mansion, a bigger boat, hearing from more and more people how wonderful you are, is just not enough.

You have to give of yourself. The one critical principle to achieving Self-Wealth and a genuine sense of fulfillment is this: You must create a goal bigger than yourself. And you must give of yourself to achieve it!

Attitude, Attitude, Attitude

To be frank, I'm not 100 percent certain why this principal works. But I can state emphatically that it does work! I've heard some religious thinkers, especially New Age practitioners, offer this explanation: we live in an orderly universe governed by spiritual law; there are no accidents, and our creator returns the money ten-fold that we share with others. Some philosophers say that our universe operates under the law of cause and effect; by giving to others we just naturally receive from others. I guess it is part of the good Karma concept some people uphold.

I suspect that it is much simpler than metaphysics or philosophy would have us believe. I believe that when we create goals bigger than ourselves, regardless of whether or not we truly believe we can achieve them, the very process gives us a tangible objective. This puts us in the right frame of mind to succeed. As for me, I can assure you that the right frame of mind or attitude was and continues to be critical for success. Ultimately, I believe success results more from attitude than ability. I know this principal works. And if it works, it works. So be it.

I suggest you accept the fact that a goal bigger than yourself is critical to ensure your success and to achieve Self–Wealth. Better yet, prove it in your own life. I'll share an example of this principle which proved very dramatic in my own life.

The $150,000 Check

Since it was my purpose, once wealthy, to make a significant impact on the lives of others, I made it known that charitable groups could approach me. I was living in Reno, Nevada in 1990, and the local president of The United Way invited me to lunch to discuss an important matter.

The Reno United Way had been unable to fund all of its commitments that year. They were $125,000 short for a hospital project, $15,000 short for an American Indian colony project they had promised to fund, and $10,000 dollars short on their funding to the Girl Scouts. In total, they needed $150,000! At that time, after taxes, I had about $160,000 in ready cash, with the rest of my money tied up in long-term programs with big penalties for early withdrawal. Instead of considering all the reasons why I couldn't afford it, I simply wrote him a check for $150,000.

Although I did not seek it nor did I expect it, the response to my contribution was astounding. The local newspaper picked up the story about my gift being the single largest United Way donation in Nevada history. I knew nothing about the article until my telephone began ringing off the wall with calls from dozens of prominent Reno and Las Vegas well wishers. The week following the donation and subsequent newspaper article was the most rewarding and heartwarming seven days of my life.

But it doesn't stop there. The next year my income increased over $1.5 million, which was a ten-fold return on my charitable donation! That gift was not only the best investment into my state of being and sense of fulfillment, but it also turned out to be the greatest financial investment I ever made.

Believe me, the serenity and fulfillment you'll receive by creating a goal bigger than yourself that requires giving of yourself, and then meeting that goal, can far exceed any financial gain. A year later I was flown to Washington, D.C. to receive the *Washington Times* "Philanthropist of the Year" award for the entire state of Nevada. I've never felt more joy than I did throughout that whole experience. It was a tremendous feeling to know that my money made a significant difference to a hospital, a Native American colony, and the Girl Scouts.

The Plausibility Factor : *Belief we're worth that much money!!*

There is another critical reason that I recommend creating a bigger goal than personal acquisition when you make your decision to achieve Self-Wealth. I call this reason the plausibility factor. One of the hardest things we face when we set a goal of how much money we want to make is the belief that we are worth that much money. Let's take a wild example and say you set a goal for yourself of $100,000 a month. Who in their right minds can convince themselves that they are worth that much money? Unless you have been raised with ten silver spoons in your mouth, that kind of money simply is not plausible. For that matter, consider the income I had arrived at not too long after I launched my first business venture. I was making $30,000 a month. I know, and you know, plenty of people for whom an income like that *per year* is difficult to obtain. Maybe you are one of them. So right

27

now you may be looking at these pages, and envisioning your pay stub and thinking "no way!"

That's where the plausibility factor comes in. If you have included in your Self-Wealth plan a specific goal of providing a significant part of your newly acquired wealth to others, and *if you passionately intend to follow through,* your motivation is far stronger. Now you can feel the tremendous need and drive within yourself to generate the high level of income you have specified in your goals.

If you can't think of any specific worthy cause that has personal significance, consider some of these: $50,000 a month will feed a village of 700 inhabitants in several desperate countries. Or that same amount will fund a prison reading and literacy program for over 10,000 inmates. Or it will fund a project that provides temporary shelter and an evening meal for every homeless person to be found in a typical American city of a quarter million people. If you were making $100,000 a month, you could commit to dealing with one of these needs quite handily and still have plenty to ensure your own freedom from want.

I use the amount of $100,000 here for its shock value, to free up your thinking. If you are reading this book, you aspire to Self-Wealth both of the spiritual and financial kind. Take the previous examples and try them out against an income of $30,000 a month. Could you spare $15,000 a month for worthwhile endeavors such as those? You bet you could! A monthly income of $15,000 buys plenty of toys, plenty of personal freedom, plenty of financial security!

Now for the sake of my argument, say that your first endeavor on the way to Self-Wealth returns you half of what mine did, or $15,000 a month. Say you made the same commitment up front to give away half your earnings toward worthwhile causes. Could you live comfortably on $7500 a month? You bet you could! Your mansion might have a few dozen less square feet, your yacht might be ten feet shorter (which would make docking fees less) and you might eat less lobster. But you would still be wealthy!

Why give away so much? Why create such a huge goal as giving away half of all you earn? Even churches only ask their devout for a tenth! My answer to this is that it's very simple. Anybody can divide by two! And setting this huge goal gives you a justifiable motive for earning truly big money. I don't believe that I am worth $100,000 a month on my own merits any more than you do. How about $25,000 a month? That's more than the median annual income of a two-adult working family. So how can one person be worth more in a week than two others are worth in a year? If you don't feel "worth" that much, you won't produce at that level.

It is a matter of having the right frame of mind. Michael Jordan, the Bulls basketball superstar, performed at a level that paid him well over a million dollars a month! He wasn't hesitant to ask for that much. Ask yourself, should he have earned more than you by playing a game most of us outgrew in adolescence? Whatever you may think about basketball as a profession for grown men, you can bet he was worth that much, or he wouldn't have earned it. And it is well known that he gives a great deal of it away.

I may never convince you that you're worth this kind of money personally. But what if an entire village of starving indigents depended on your efforts? Well, there are plenty of just causes in need of the money you can earn! So when you sit down at the outset of your new entrepreneurial life to write down objectives, be bold. Establish first and foremost that your Self-Wealth will be used to positively and dramatically impact others. This makes the need for such amounts plausible. The earnings you specify will become justified to your worst critic: yourself. The years my co-authors and I have spent as "entrepreneurial coaches" have driven home to us the importance of helping aspiring entrepreneurs to fully understand this goal-oriented approach. Your goal must be something larger than yourself, of benefit to many, and clearly articulated. The amount you write down as your target income then becomes a means to your ends, not the end in itself.

It's Not All Just Football

Consider the story of Art Williams. I first heard about Art Williams when he was a football coach in a small rural community. Even then, his name came up in post-game bar talk in the same sentence as my personal coaching hero, Vince Lombardi. Young Art Williams was a motivator who could bring out the best in his kids, and did. What I didn't know during his coaching days was that fermenting beneath the surface of that high school coach was a long-standing desire to give battle to a specific industry whose practices had unfairly resulted in an impoverished childhood—his own.

In and around the insurance industry today, Art Williams has attained the status of a folk hero of such proportions that most of his admirers and many of his most ardent detractors agree as to the huge influence he has had within the insurance industry. Though prompted by his own impoverished childhood, Art Williams subscribed to the Self-Wealth principle of creating a goal bigger than himself.

Art Williams lost his father to premature death when he was a young boy. The large family was left destitute. As Art later found out, much of their financial plight could have been avoided. His father's best friend was an insurance salesman, and his father had trusted his friend to secure adequate life insurance coverage to protect his family in the event of his untimely death.

But his friend didn't advise Mr. Williams to invest what little money he had for insurance into a "term" life policy with a large face amount. Art's father was guided into purchasing a small "whole-life" policy with little or no early death benefit. As an adult, Art Williams studied the life insurance industry to see what had happened. One factor never quite made sense to him. Why were agents selling "whole-life" policies with small early death benefits to young families at precisely the time they might most need more revenue in the event of the breadwinner's premature demise?

Then one day Art overheard the "shop talk" of some veteran insurance agents. He learned that the bonus paid to agents on "whole life" policies with little early-death protection was 55 percent, compared to only 20 percent for "term" policies, which would have paid far more to survivors of early deaths. The veteran agents were cynically far more interested in their higher commissions than providing the protection so desperately needed by young families.

Art Williams got mad. Extremely mad. But he channeled his anger into the most constructive channel he could envision. He founded his own independent insurance company to offer term life to just the kind of families his had been when his father died. In a very short time, his crusading young agents were selling more "term" life insurance in one year than New York Life, and Metropolitan combined. Those companies are each over 100 years

31

old! When I read a chapter in Art's book on "Crusades" I found myself cheering like a schoolchild. Eventually, he sold his company, but not before teaching the world an object lesson in creating Self-Wealth via angry integrity. More importantly, and the lesson applicable to my argument here, is that Art Williams prospered because he had a crusade, a goal bigger than himself.

A Passionate Goal Bigger Than Yourself

A few words about anger: anger need never lead to verbal, emotional, mental, or physical abuse. As you master the tenets of Self-Wealth, you will learn to convert righteous anger into productive activity under just the right circumstances, for just the right reasons.

Here's an example of using anger creatively. My co-authors and I have had opportunities to deliver countless lectures and speeches in numerous countries. From corporate "Rah! Rah!" sessions to serious fiscal strategic planning and land reform meetings, we've had many opportunities to speak to large groups. Upon one occasion, an invitation to speak—and the requested topic— provoked my personal ire.

The occasion was a high school commencement speech in a city in Indiana. I was solicited to give the keynote graduation speech to 487 graduates. What disturbed me was the demeanor of the principle. From the outset, she didn't want to talk about her graduates. Instead, she spoke of the spirit of the local PTA, the selfless parents who worked as substitute teachers, often at their own economic loss, the great new computers donated by two local corporations, and the wondrous psychological skills used by the faculty to whip these little ragamuffins into shape. These were the things she wanted me to focus on in my address.

Because her attitude angered me, I accepted her invitation on the spot. When the big night came, the 1450-seat football stands were filled to the top. Every one of the principal's bragged-about contributors appeared to be there to feel proud of themselves.

Here was my opening: "You 487 young graduates are more intelligent, more worthy, more empathetic and will be much, much greater than any of your relatives sitting here tonight. You can do and be anything you wish and shame on you if you pick their choice of life paths for you over your own. You're at your peak. Were it not so, there would be no such thing as natural selection or evolution and yet we all know that progress has resulted from generations leap-frogging past their progenitors.

> *"Any group of laborers can build a stadium this size in less than a year, but you have each built a great human being in 18 years all by yourself with a bit of guidance and probably a few divine interventions...."*

At the conclusion of the speech, the only standing ovation came from the 487 kids on the front rows. But here's the rest of the story. Two days after graduation an extremely angry CPA phoned me with news that his valedictorian daughter had declined to join his accounting firm. She was going to enter art school, her real love. He ranted, he raved, he cursed and even threatened to sue before he slammed down the phone.

Three months later, helping the CPA's daughter pack for art school, her mother found a suicide note that accidentally fell from an obscure purse. The young woman had already written the note,

33

and planned a summer suicide following graduation. She would have rather died young than face what to her was the slow death of a career in accounting.

My phone rang again. As they wept over the phone, recounting this story to me and making amends for the earlier rudeness, I understood we'd just seen the magic of positive anger in all its splendor. Anger-driven goals bigger than ourselves, even as in this case, when it is simply a speech articulating them, can literally become life and death matters. From my perspective of true Self-Wealth, sending those young people away from commencement with a full head of self-esteem was significantly more critical than elevating the stature of their elders or predicting their futures.

By the way, the closing 17 words of the graduation speech were attributed to Confucius centuries ago. "Choose a job you love, and you will never have to work another day in your life."

If you are serious about Self-Wealth, pause right now. Consider the decisions of that high-school senior. And commit those 17 words from Confucius to memory! Post them on your workspace! *Remember them!*

Out of Your Comfort Zone

In the new millennium it will no longer be tenable for us to "stuff" our emotions. We are going to need to follow the Al Williams example; that is, we are going to have to begin looking at the inequities in our world and use our anger constructively to deal with them. Let the old "think and grow rich" cry of the past be replaced with "Act and grow balanced."

Self-Wealth will begin in earnest when hitherto armchair quarterbacks awaken to the plight of others on this planet. It isn't a pretty sight: all the homelessness, indigent alcoholics, greed, unwed mothers, functionally illiterate high school graduates, underfunded charitable institutions, familial abuse and deprivation, drug pushers inside elementary school gates...ethnic cleansing, preventable famines—the list seems to go on and on.

Self-Wealth is not for the faint-hearted glutton. Sacrifices are as much a part of the equation as acquisitions, accolades, rewards, and edification. In the end, Self-Wealth balances self-sacrifice with material abundance; the result is countless "win-wins." We need to get angry about the fact that there are still so many win/lose players out there. Right now, let's consult our own mirrors a bit and view life less globally, less societally and more from a personal vantage point. There are some seemingly silly little things about ourselves that should anger us a bit and serve to stimulate our march toward Self-Wealth.

Here are some things about which perhaps we should become somewhat angry, or at least irritated.

Look how routine we allow our lives to become. We are either like emotionless robots on a treadmill or like agitated, caged lions, pacing back and forth back and forth, in the cages of our own making. Does it not anger you to realize that you take exactly the same route each day to your destination? Is it because it's the fastest? Is it because it was the fastest 20 years ago, and you haven't checked alternatives lately? Is expediency always your norm? Why not try six new routes to work or anywhere you regularly travel? Go ahead, try it for six days. See what fortuitous intersections offer themselves up when you are open to the possibility. Get angry about your mundane routines. Change them as a first positive step

35

toward diversity, new goals, fortuitous intersections, and Self-Wealth.

Get angry when you see 50 wealthy people in a row pass a beggar with a cup on a cold winter night in your city. So what if the five bucks you give him aren't spent on a hot meal? That's *his* choice. Your choice is to answer the need he clearly has; you *are* your brother's keeper! If not you, who?

Get angry about your consistent avoidance of adrenaline sports. Take up paragliding. Go bungy jumping. Go white-water rafting down the middle fork of the Salmon River for a week in the majestic wilderness. Learn to fly a bi-plane. There's not a lot of adrenaline in marching around a manicured pasture in pink half-pants beating up a little white ball. To "Putt or To Soar," that is the question. Golf is phenomenal, but so are other pursuits.

Anger at any of the above facets of life, positively directed, can facilitate an entire personality change and image boost for any Self-Wealth aspirant. For too long this emotion called anger has been disrespected, ignored, suppressed or mis-expressed.

The Self-Wealth Equation

We believe in a simple equation: PA + PA = SW. Positive anger plus practical application equals Self-Wealth.

What does all this equation, and positive anger, have to do with a goal bigger than yourself? Simple. Complacency, routine, and comfort zones will not move you. Until you are consciously shocked into recognizing that the world is passing you by, until you become cognizant of the fact that most folks' mottoes are "full speed astern," inertia will continue to rule your life. I got my shock, my "wake-up" call, in April of 1986. What will it take to awaken *you* to the possibilities of Self-Wealth?

Before moving on to the next chapter, take some time to create a goal much bigger than yourself. Look around your community and see what needs doing. If you are unmoved by local philanthropic possibilities, take a look at the global situation. You shouldn't have any trouble figuring out ways to share your wealth. Make certain that you dream big, and make sure that you have an emotional investment in your goal. The more you can relate to the specific cause, the more you'll work toward that goal. Please don't skip this step. Frequently, when would-be entrepreneurs call my co-authors and me to assert that our system isn't working, we simply ask them one question: "What goal bigger than yourself did you set?" Often the failing entrepreneur has skipped this step.

Trust me on this one. If you have no legitimate reason for earning $100,000 a month, or whatever figure you select, you *will not earn that much*. You will not think the right way. You will not be able to think big enough. You will automatically limit yourself and your earning potential. You will not become wealthy, either internally or externally.

Application

To complete this chapter, please participate in the following exercise.

1. As a child what observation of unfairness, abuse or rotten behavior of any kind angered you? Write it down in detail.

2. If not as a child, as an adolescent or adult, have you ever seen an inequity occur either in real life or on television that angered you? Write it down in detail.

Now, go find out how, armed with $50,000 extra each month you might impact one of those problems. If you can only give 50 cents now, give it! Then create a real goal bigger than yourself, write it down, read and visualize it every day. Say it aloud! "My goal is to..." Set sub goals that you can achieve en route to the larger objective. "Today I will..."

CHAPTER 2

Bungy Jumping With Rattlesnakes:

Self-Mastery Experiences are the Cornerstone

"You gain strength, courage and confidence by every experience in which you really stop to look fear in the face. You are able to say to yourself, "I lived through this. I can take the next thing that comes along. You must do the thing you think you cannot do."

Eleanor Roosevelt

A necessary step toward Self-Wealth is the development of self-mastery. Self-mastery is the inherent capacity you have to control your thoughts and actions, and to go about life with confidence. It is when you do not feel that you are in control, or that in some way you don't feel confident enough to take action, that you are lacking in self-mastery. We are the masters of our own destinies. Self-mastery is a matter of recognizing this, and acting upon it with confidence.

If you are feeling blocked and inadequate in your life now, has there ever been a time when you didn't? I'm betting there is. It may well have been when you were a child, before life's disappointments began to weigh you down. One simple exercise is to think back, find those incidents of self-mastery, those times when you were in control and recognized your self-confidence, and experience again the feelings you knew when you achieved that wonderful state.

I was very lucky as a youngster not only to experience opportunities for self-mastery, but also to perceive them as such. Each challenge I overcame left me with a feeling of confidence to face ensuing challenges. Let me relate a story of mine to you now. Use it to plumb your memory for stories of your own, and then explore how you feel about those stories now. Does the sense of self-mastery and confidence return? Do you disregard those feelings as irrelevant to your present sense of frustration? Or, worst of all, do you minimize your own success as a one-time lucky break and vow never to take a risk again?

Here is my story.

Bat Hell

At age 10 several of my buddies and I discovered a rather large cave on the shores of the James River near the Missouri farmlands where I spent my childhood. The cave had a relatively small entrance through which we had to crawl. This opened into a large chamber with tunnels branching out from each wall. It was a child's fantasy to go spelunking in that particular cave. We always took plenty of water, rolls of yarn and flashlights in order to feel we had "survival" gear.

During one of our regular summer afternoon forays into the cave I discovered a rather obscure passageway above us in the chamber ceiling. I was just tall enough, once hoisted on a friend's shoulders, to get a handhold and climb up into the overhead tunnel. Once inside I was astounded at the size of the overhead chamber, fully twice as large as the one below. I began shouting about my exciting discovery, but wasn't able to entice my buddies up through the ceiling with me.

I set out on my own, laying out string behind me, to explore the new tunnels leading off the overhead chamber. Most were dead ends, but one led a considerable distance before it opened into a huge chamber that reeked of ammonia. A sweep of my flashlight across the ceiling disclosed hundreds of bats beginning to stir, a sight which caused me to attempt a hasty retreat from "Bat Hell."

In my haste I slipped on the bat droppings and pitched my flashlight, shattering the lens and bulb. I was now in much feared total darkness. Worse, I knew there was a six-foot drop somewhere in the floor behind me, which I would have to safely find to escape and rejoin my pals. I didn't know until next morning that they had left me behind to get to their respective homes in time for supper. It never occurred to them that I might encounter problems. Besides, to a 10-year-old, a friend's safety shrinks to insignificance when compared to potential parental anger if we are late for dinner.

Alone, I decided my best strategy was to kneel down and grope slowly for the hole and then carefully drop through it feet first. But in the dark, my reaching hand found empty space and I fell through the hole. I landed on my back and got the wind knocked out of me. As I lay there gasping for oxygen, I frantically wiggled all my limbs to make certain that nothing was broken or sprained. When I was ready to move again, it occurred to me that among the eight or ten tunnels toward which I was going to have to grope and experiment, only one crawl space led outside. Several of the dead ends were very long and narrow. How to choose? I began yelling frantically for my friends, to no avail. As it sank in that they were gone, I crawled toward a random wall in search of the first tunnel.

To my relief, I saw shadows cast by the sunset at the very end of the first crawl space I discovered. I couldn't believe my luck. I crawled rapidly toward the fading light. The tunnel bent slightly up and to the right, and became significantly tighter than I remembered it. Nevertheless, I reasoned, it had to be the entrance. It wasn't.

With both arms stretched before me, I was pulling myself along literally by my fingers, when my left knee became lodged against a small rock behind me. I couldn't move my body in any direction. Full-blown panic set in when I realized I couldn't move forward or backward. I was lodged in a cave tunnel approximately four feet from the tiny opening, couldn't turn around and couldn't go forward. At that age I couldn't even spell claustrophobia—but at that precise moment, I could have told you exactly what it was, if I could have spoken.

Even then, in that predicament, my brain was processing three things that kept my mental outlook teetering on the right side of sanity. First, I had enough oxygen, because the cave opening was so close. Second, the longest I could remain trapped was one night, because I could shout to the regular morning fishermen, and they would immediately come to my rescue. Third, it was summer, and, in spite of the damp coolness of the cave, I was close enough to the opening to stay warm.

I was doing a fine job of managing my phobia when the first angry bat banged against the sole of my tennis shoe. I had inadvertently chosen the bats' exit from the cave, and it was evening feeding time.

All rational thought fled.

I was wedged between a thousand bats and their meals. My mind ran wild with images. What if they started climbing up my pant legs in a furious attempt to escape? How many were rabid like dad always said bats were? Forget rabies! How long would it take me to bleed to death from a million little teeth gnawing on my ankles and calves? I began to lose it.

With every fiber of my being, utilizing every fingernail and ounce of strength in my toes, I attempted to force myself backwards. On the second try I felt some progress. Next effort, two more hard-fought inches. I was backing out! I would beat the bats. Slowly, agonizingly, I inched backward until I found space to turn around. In that moment I heard the fluttering of hundreds of hairless wings. But they weren't all over me. For the first time it occurred to me that the bats had chosen the exit I had sought as their alternate route. As the last bats left the cave I needed only follow the rustle of their departure to find my way out.

Within fifteen minutes I was outside riding my bicycle toward home. The summer wind was in my hair, and—my relief was overcome by an enormous sense of personal achievement and self-mastery. I had prevailed!

Self–Wealth

Overcoming Fears & Changing Your Life

In this chapter I want to spend a little time exploring the advantage of overcoming phobias in one area of your life which automatically leads to benefits in other areas of your life.

Cognitive clinical studies during the last few years of the twentieth century verified a remarkable fact: when someone challenges and ultimately overcomes a deep-seated fear, the resulting confidence has a "spill-over" effect. For me, I have developed a sort of fearless attitude for things in life. Each time I overcame a fear, I discovered that I had fewer fears to overcome. It is what has enabled me to succeed and to help others succeed. You develop a "Can do!" attitude by challenging your fears. And when I'm not taking business risks (or other physically "tame" challenges), I now keep myself pumped by engaging in peak performance sports and adrenaline rushing activities like bungy jumping or paragliding that defy fear. This is the essence of self-mastery: to overcome your fears, to build confidence, and to be more effective in your life.

Dr. Albert Bandura of Stanford University discusses the phenomenon at length in his remarkable book *Self-Efficacy: The Exercise of Control.* He and other psychologists worked to help individuals overcome snake phobias. During follow up counseling sessions, they discovered tremendous peripheral benefits. Those who had successfully overcome their fear of snakes tended to live life more boldly in other areas of their lives. Several had taken up public speaking—an endeavor maybe marginally less frightful to most than snake-handling. Others had terminated counterproductive marriages, changed jobs, or accomplished a host of other activities normally associated with extreme anxiety.

44

These researchers discovered that the link between conquering the initial phobia and the other behaviors was quantitatively significant. Investigations into the phenomenon were launched by several other respected researchers. All of them confirmed the premise that confronting and conquering personal phobias have definite and positive "spill-over" into other areas of life.

Our Fear of Noises & Heights

Psychologists inform us that children are born with only two inherent phobias: fear of loud noises and fear of heights. When loud noises usually prove to be more of an irritant than actually dangerous, that fear wanes. But by age one, most of us have confirmed our fear of heights by a few tumbles in which gravity resulted in pain. As we then progress through adolescence and adulthood the fear of heights never leaves us. Higher and higher heights tend to be quite disturbing. Most people never bungy jump because leaping from a point several hundred feet above the earth seems mad. It's just the old phobia at work. When I bungy-jumped in New Zealand, the adrenaline rush was wonderful! I admit, at first, I had my share of trepidation. But I got over it.

Heights don't bother me now, they thrill me. As a hang-glider and ultra-light pilot, I can assure you there's nothing more thrilling than soaring with the eagles and hawks at cloud base. People from all over the world stop to photograph us as we launch our paragliders and hang-gliders above Lake Tahoe. Invariably one of the observers will comment that he can't even imagine the lure of such a dangerous sport. I've overheard fragments of conversations like "death wish" and "they're idiots" on numerous occasions. Why? That same old phobia; people who have always feared heights and simply cannot imagine why we no longer do. By denigrating us, they rationalize their phobia. Such a failure to examine different thought processes, even thought processes that may seem extreme to you right now, can only lead to failure in your trek toward Self-Wealth.

To achieve anything meaningful in this life usually runs against the grain. You have to think differently and more extremely than most everyone to surpass most everyone. Overachievers are not people who are content to merely accept things as they are, they challenge themselves and everyone in the world around them. This is an important key to experiencing a life of Self-Wealth.

Overcoming Your Fears by Physical Means

The Self-Wealth principles I am offering are something you can put into effect today. There is no need to wait. If you are serious about making a change in your life now, you can take some real actions now to get the process going. Developing self-mastery skills is an important step towards experiencing Self-Wealth. Self-mastery with respect to overcoming fears, such as the fear of heights, or snakes, or other challenges, is a good place to start to facilitate change in your life.

However, having said this, it would not be prudent or fair for me to avoid mentioning the inherent risks involved in such daring activities as bungy jumping, snake handling, hang gliding, or other comparably dangerous endeavors. Because the fact is that even in the presence of experts, trained therapists, or peak-performance gurus, there's still the chance of fear, injury or death. If you fear heights,

running off a mountain with one of the greatest tandem paragliding experts in America, like Ray Leonard of Adventure Sports in Carson City, Nevada, could still terrify you. Injury could result. Bungy jumping is a peak-performance experience, but bungy chords do occasionally break.

When I encourage you to participate, understand that ultimately it is your choice and your choice alone. Were such experiences not inherently dangerous, it's questionable whether they would be sufficiently challenging to quality as self-mastery experiences.

Of course there are other self-mastery experiences which do not involve obvious or physical danger. Ultimately self-mastery involves the exercise of courage. For a woman it could be the life changing "everyday" events like giving birth to a child, for others it could be staying a difficult course to keep promises we've made. Many people build self-mastery when they challenge the halls of higher learning. Some self-mastery experiences in life are like running a marathon (itself a self-mastery experience) which tests a person's courage.

If you're like me and are inclined to try the physically exciting stuff, please prepare with an expert. Sign the disclaimers, and be willing to accept responsibility for your own outcome. Choose to face your phobias head on. I believe that the benefits of mastery experiences far outweigh the dangers. Self-Wealth as I define it is not about "thinking and growing rich." It's about doing and achieving. The odds that you will eventually die are one out of one. What I am concerned about in my approach to Self-Wealth is that you do not die without ever having fully lived.

Self-Mastery Activity List

I have already recommended several physical means to challenge yourself starting right now, with the aim to overcome fears and develop self-mastery.

Here is my favorite list of self-mastery experiences available to us all:

Tandem paragliding with a certified instructor
Bungy jumping with a professional company
Tandem skydiving with a certified skydiving expert
Snow boarding
Ice/indoor climbing with an experienced climber
Snake handling with a trained therapist
Adventure flying with a certified, small plane pilot
Spelunking with cave experts
High swing experiences at reputable amusement areas
Race car driving at reputable schools
Public speaking at Toastmaster Organizations
Outward Bound experiences with an adventure company
White water rafting with professional guides and outfitting companies.

Each of these endeavors is not without risk, but when experienced with trained professionals, the risks are significantly reduced. The serious student of Self-Wealth will confront his or her phobias early on in the process of achievement. Again, I assure you that the benefits far outweigh the dangers. We have personally recommended these and similar experiences to serious students of Self-Wealth, and have personally participated in many without incident. I would send my own elderly parents on such adventures without concern for their well being. I let my daughter go handgliding with Ray Leonard when she was merely fifteen years old.

You cannot afford to treat life as a spectator sport and hope to achieve the life I advocate in this book. If some of the recommendations seem beyond the scope of your ability—great! Twenty-first century Self-Wealth will not be accomplished through "thinking" only but through mastery experiences involving thought, action, courage, and much more. If my suggestions frighten you, they should! If they render you immobile, that's your old "comfort zone" kicking in. That's maybe how you got stalled in the first place. My colleagues and I won't accept responsibility for your decision to participate in such activities, but I can assure you that failure to do so can leave your life boring, mundane and frustrating. It's all up to you. Escape mediocrity and TAKE ACTION! Immediately! Time is of the essence!

Spirituality Augments Self-Mastery

While many say my approach to Self-Wealth tends to have a secular humanist bent, there are spiritual and philosophical elements

49

to the Self-Wealth principles. I believe your spirituality, spiritual side, psyche—whatever you choose to call it, can help you come to terms with your fears as effectively as actual physical experiences, or as I call them, "cognitive mastery experiences." In dealing with fear, there are several decidedly spiritual approaches that can enable you to overcome fear and accelerate self-mastery.

A number of historical theologians agree with the Apostle Paul in his frequently quoted comment, "as a man thinketh in his heart, so is he." Theological writings often acknowledge and discuss the unique unlimited potential of each individual. I believe that countless references in theological thinking refer to imagery, visualization and meditation. These spiritually oriented techniques are critical components in the process of achieving Self-Wealth.

Spiritual Techniques

At the very least there are two techniques you should adopt: meditation combined with visualizations. I also think affirmations, which lead to actualization, should be considered.

To facilitate your ability to achieve mastery over debilitating fears, professionals often offer a number of meditative techniques, and sometimes actually prayer itself, depending on the client's belief system. The devout Christian who is afraid of snakes takes considerable comfort and empowerment from prayers before the mastery experience.

Let me briefly take you through the basics of meditation and visualization.

Power Meditation

Meditation is not airy-fairy stuff. Most simply, meditation is a means to improve concentration and to experience relaxation of the mind and body. But meditation can have important, far-reaching effects in all aspects of your life. For instance, many who regularly practice simple meditation enjoy improved physical health and health awareness—and hey, the healthier you are, the easier that skydive or white water rafting trip is going to be! For me, though, the most interesting, helpful aspect of meditation is the effect it has on your brain. As you meditate, your alpha brain waves, which are the waves associated with relaxation, are stimulated. The result is a mind which is consistently in a state of a sort of "restful alertness," which some research indicates tends to enhance your creativity, comprehension, and reaction time. (This is perhaps what some refer to when they speak of "being in the present moment" or "present time.") It is a state in which your thinking becomes clearer, and it is easier to focus on the immediate tasks at hand.

Of course, the state of your brain spills over into what we call your "state of mind" and your attitude, which have been shown to effect your physical body.

Above and beyond that, you become more aware of your spiritual connections. Dr. Herbert Benson, best-selling author of *The Relaxation Response*, writes, "Meditation nourishes a feeling of connectedness to the Divine." The Divine is something somehow greater than yourself and, I assume, can be whatever you want to call it, God, Allah, Mother Mary, Jesus or your own personally meaningful divinity.

To practice meditation, a word used in the Bible 21 times, first find and set aside a private area in your home where you know you will not be disturbed. Some people find a room, a corner of a room, or a closet that they designate as their sacred meditation area.

You should also decide on a time during the day when you may be less likely to be disturbed. For some, morning or evening just before or after bed, are the best times for meditation. Decide what is best for you.

You may also have to unplug phones, turn off answering machines, alert other family members, and possibly keep pets away to ensure you get the peace and time you need, but try to establish and keep a special place and time set aside specifically for meditation.

To begin, try the so-called "concentration meditation" method. First, sit down in a chair or sit comfortably crossed legged on the floor. I don't recommend lying down, particularly if you are prone to falling asleep when you assume a horizontal position. Rest your hands comfortably on your knees or on your lap. Now, close your eyes and focus your attention on your breathing. You can also focus on a single sound (with eyes closed) or on a single object (with a relaxed gaze). I think just focusing on your breath keeps things simple.

What you are going to try to do is let all the mental static that is a constant distraction fall away. You want to still your mind. At first, thoughts, feelings, images, sounds, memories will attempt to occupy your mind as you concentrate on emptying it. Observe each, and let it go. Return to your quiet center. You want to let yourself become calm and relaxed. By breathing slowly, deeply, and in a regular, continuous flow, your mind calms.

Your breath is the key tool enabling you to transform your state of mind. Inhale deeply and gently into your abdomen; neck and shoulders relaxed. Notice as the air expands your abdomen, ribs, and, lastly, through the chest. After inhaling, gently hold the breath for a count of three. Actually say in your head: "One, two, three." Release the air slowly, exhaling from your chest downward in one, steady, silent breath. At the end of exhale, say another count of three in your head, and inhale as before. This simple breath repetition continues, steadily and gently, throughout your session.

You should practice with good posture, without slouching shoulders or rounded back. Sitting in a cross-legged position enables the breath to flow more smoothly and easily. It is the practice of concentrating on your breathing and correct posture, that keeps your mind from drifting and chatter.

So try inhaling and exhaling as described. The moment you notice that you become distracted with mind chatter or any other thoughts, correct yourself by simply taking your focus back to the breath.

Try to make your sessions about 10 to 15 minutes once a day. As you progress, you may want to meditate a couple of times a day or for longer periods. Eventually, you will find it easier to focus and concentrate. Over the course of days and weeks, as you continue to practice this simple form of meditation, you will notice how calm and keenly aware you become as you go about daily tasks.

When you are truly fully aware (conscious) of all that you do, you will find it easier to recognize and take responsibility for your actions. We do a lot of things without being fully conscious of the fact that we do them, let alone why. As a result of your meditation practice, you may more clearly recognize irrational fears that you have, relationships that serve neither you nor the person with whom you have the relationship, or any other pattern or habit that is not in your best interest. The list is endless and works for identifying the positive as well as the negative in your life.

Self-Wealth

Conscious behavior resulting from meditation will be an integral part of what leads you to Self-Wealth. As you understand Self-Wealth concepts and techniques, the state of mind meditation promotes will help you recognize, take responsibility for, and change your patterns and choices that do not serve you in your quest. This applies to any other area of your life where you might not be fully practicing what you preach or believe.

Visualization

Visualization is a powerful tool that helps you achieve your goals by training your subconscious mind to believe mental pictures of what specifically you want to achieve in reality.

Consider your desire to make a certain income level per month. This is part of your overall Self-Wealth plan to make enough money to live as you choose and finance whatever altruistic endeavor that is important to you. Close your eyes and imagine (visualize) what your life will be like. Imagine where you will live, the things you will be doing, the people with whom you will be in contact, and so on.

Make these pictures as specific and realistic as possible. Feel, see, hear, taste, smell every situation. This is very important. Though it may seem difficult at first, as you practice, your visualizations will become clearer and more specific; more realistic.

You only need to do this for a few seconds every day, perhaps during a quiet moment in the morning or before you go to bed. However, I suggest that the most powerful visualizations will occur as you meditate.

Some people use visualization to picture their goals of the near future, such as the way things may occur during the course of the coming day or week. Some use visualizations to help conquer the fears they have of their actual physical self-mastery experiences, such as snake handling or sky diving.

Whatever you visualize, it is important that you do two things: have as clear and specific a mental picture as you can in your mind, and go about your life feeling as though and acting as if (in attitude) what you visualize has already happened. If you visualize having achieved a certain level of success, start to act with the confidence you feel during your visualizations of having reached that level.

By thinking a goal, visualizing that goal, and going about life as though you have already achieved that goal, the chances are greater that you will actually achieve that goal. It's a self-fulfilling prophecy sort of thing.

Those who use visualization as an integral part of their successful lives tend to make things happen to themselves, and draw to them things or people which make things happen with respect to their goals.

Why? Visualization effects attitude which effects outcome. Their subconscious minds are prepared for success and they know they can take action when they have to. Consequently, they eventually succeed.

Being happy, healthful and experiencing life to its fullest with serenity and balance is something you have to *make* happen. Anyone can use visualization as a way of making things happen, and I encourage you to give it a try for all goals in your life.

Affirmations

Visualization proves that what you think about can have a dramatic effect on your life. Be aware that the words you say are just as important.

Words have power. Words have the power to make better, to encourage, to nurture, and words also have the power to destroy. As you go about seeking to develop your self-mastery skills and practicing Self-Wealth principles, keep in mind words that empower and to encourage you. Getting fit in mind, body, and soul is much easier if we are encouraged. We must draw on all sources of empowerment to help us achieve our goals.

It is a fact that actually saying words and phrases aloud to yourself effects your mind and your body. This is neurolinguistics. Affirmations are one way of making sure those effects are positive and helpful, by using positive, empowering words and feelings and thoughts.

For example, you can say aloud to yourself:
"I am going to create a monthly income five times what I make now!"

To bring about the means to achieve your goal, say this now to yourself and continue as you go about your daily activities. By making that statement, you are making a subconscious commitment.

Your conscious mind can *decide* what you want to say. Your subconscious mind, on the other hand, just records what you say or think, positive or negative. What your subconscious mind believes (what you consciously tell it as the truth) will automatically effect other aspects of your life. When you subconsciously believe that you are going to succeed in a specific way, you actually develop the confidence and attitude that leads to opportunities, ideas, contacts with the appropriate people, and so on, to achieve your goal.

When I began my network marketing business, failure was not an option. Each day I told myself "I will make this happen. I will contact such and so number of people. Others have made it happen before me, and I can make it happen now. I did it yesterday, and I can do it today."

By consciously making these statements to myself, my subconscious was empowered with the attitude to achieve my goals, long-range, short-term, and daily. Armed with a great attitude, my goals became reality.

Repeating positive phrases out loud to yourself may not seem like much on the surface. But once you try it, you will discover that affirmations are a very effective way of achieving things in your life, and actually make things easier.

Use the following affirmations as a way to generally improve your attitude:

"I will succeed at all that I do."

"I will not let challenges stand in the way of my success."

"I may feel discouraged at times, but that is only a temporary emotion."

"I press forward no matter what happens."

Create your own affirmations of self-encouragement and nurturing. The point is to begin thinking positively as much as possible, and always choose active, vivid, present-tense words for your affirmations.

Simply putting a smile on your face is another form of affirmation. Again, this may seem simple and naïve, but it works. When something happens to make you discouraged or frustrated, just decide that it is okay, and smile to yourself and everyone else. After all, whatever discouraged you or made you frustrated in the past became now will become of little importance in a year or two. So, why make it such a big deal now?

Just try it, and you can see how it can work.

Advantages of Spiritual Techniques

Spiritual techniques empower you emotionally, spiritually and mentally to overcome your fears, frustrations, and any discouragement you may feel, and arm you with a positive attitude. They enable you to overcome your fears and boost your confidence from the inside. Cultivating your spiritual side gives you the opportunity for serenity in all areas of your life. When all areas of your life get careful attention, the result is balance, and that is fundamental to the Self-Wealth experience.

God Shines His Face

I always felt that God's face shined on me from a very early age; that lady luck had paid me a crib-side visit. Nearly everything I have done in my life has worked to my advantage. Granted, I have had my share of misfortunes and personal challenges, such as my first marriage, my challenge with alcohol, and my inauspicious experience as a minister, and so on. But even with these bumps of life I always found a way, sooner or later, to surmount problems and obstacles.

Indeed, I always grew stronger, more resourceful, became more confident, and generally made the best of life.

Over the course of my life I have always sought to learn from others. I studied people who had dealt with challenges in their own lives, and managed to get through them victoriously. I learned to emulate those who were successful. I also strive to deal head on with my fears and my shortcomings. Every time I put my mind, body, and soul into something, I always succeed. I remember when I first began to speak before groups of people. For most people, public speaking can be one of the most terrifying experiences of all, perhaps even more terrifying than bungy jumping or sky diving. For me, it was no different than most people. But I was determined to overcome the fear of speaking publicly. I challenged myself. I simply wanted to see if I could do it.

So, as I have done with just about everything else in my life, I read everything I could get my hands on about public speaking and speech making, and even began attending as many speeches as I could in order to learn how to do it. Eventually, I started making speeches at the local Kiwanis and Rotary clubs. After doing a few speeches I built my confidence, developed my speech, and made speeches regularly for a variety of venues. Before long, I was receiving invitations to speak. Within a couple of years I was making several thousand dollars per speech. Years later I even wrote a book on the subject called *Power Speaking*.

The point here is the two things I did to overcome my fear of public speaking: I studied other people who succeeded in this area and then I took the necessary baby steps—I started small, gradually speaking to larger and larger groups. Nothing really happens overnight. Before too long, I not only overcame the fear, but I got so good at speaking that I started to make some serious money as a professional speaker. Today, I make many dozens of speeches each year as part of my effort to help people achieve their full potential. I never allowed a fear to paralyze me from doing something. I never once said, "I'm afraid of this, so I can't do it." I have always said, "I can do this if I put myself into it."

In business, I had an experience similar to my public speaking experience. Before I entered business, my working skills and experiences were limited to the social sciences and theology. I certainly had no business acumen or education. Yet, despite all my apparent disadvantages, I studied how others succeeded and learned to duplicate their efforts. This helped me build confidence and success. I am absolutely convinced that this is at least part of why I achieved an income in excess of a million dollars a year in my very first entrepreneurial venture.

My approach led to success in areas other than finances as well. I have excelled in music, hang-gliding competitions, and racquetball, though I never received formal training in any of those areas. I always found a way to work things out, both on my own and with the assistance of others—sometimes with a combination of the two.

Yes, God's face shined on me. The manner in which He blessed me was the gift of my willingness to challenge myself to learn, to take chances, and to overcome my fears.

I "stumbled" into these principles of success by trial, error, and instinct. I really did not know what I was doing. In fact, it was not until many years later through my exposure to Dr. Bandura's book, *Self-Efficacy*, that I recognized the underlying reason for the realization of Self-Wealth in my life.

Self Mastery: Natural or Iduced

It is interesting that throughout my relatively unsupervised youth, I wound up in a number of situations similar to my adventure of the bat cave, and in every one, the lesson I took from it was that I could prevail. It was those situations that resulted in the confidence which would later allow me to capitalize on countless opportunities in life. Far from luck, my adult ability to capitalize and create Self-Wealth was a direct result of having experienced many self-mastery situations in my childhood. They can be just as easily created as an adult.

It is remarkable to me now when I realize that such self-mastery can be achieved either in the course of normal life experiences (as I had), or deliberately induced (through cognitive mastery experiences and spiritual techniques) as aptly demonstrated by Dr. Bandura and his colleagues and numerous theologins. Each self-mastery experience, whether "natural" or induced, results in ancillary benefits. It is exciting to know that, right now, opportunities abound for personal growth for anyone. You don't have to wait for the opportunity to make a change in your life. You can participate in a self-mastery experience today.

Application Exercise

Respond to the following questions in writing as a way to help you to take action now in your effort to experience self-mastery:

1. What are the 5-10 greatest challenges you have overcome in your life? How did they build self-mastery?

2. What fear are you going to overcome in the next few months?

Dentist,

3. What fear must you overcome in order to achieve the goal greater than yourself which you determined in the first chapter?

CHAPTER 3

All I Believe I Am, I Am:

Self-Efficacy: Erasing Self-Doubt

"I am all I have, to work with, to play with to suffer and to enjoy. It is not the eyes of others that I am wary of but my own. I do not intend to let myself down more than I can possibly help, and I find that the fewer illusions I have about me or the world around me, the better company I am for myself."

Noel Coward

Barry Sefton had no formal training as a mechanic, but Barry could perform wonders on any motorcycle engine that fell into his chunky 23-year-old hands. My colleague and co-author, John Radford, got to know Barry after John reassembled his 1964 Honda

Goldwing motorcycle engine and discovered the amateur mechanic's worst fear: there on the workshop floor lay an engine part; maybe a critical component of the gearbox. After approaching all the local motorcycle dealers, John was none the wiser. He couldn't risk starting the motor. That's when Barry Sefton came to the rescue.

Barry arrived one evening wearing his back-to-front cap, and studied the orphaned part briefly, pushed the motorcycle a few feet with the gears engaged and with the motor turned off. He then made the surprising announcement:

"This part does not belong to this motorcycle!"

The Honda never missed a beat in the subsequent six years John owned it.

Mastery of internal combustion machines would be enough for many. But as John came to know Barry, while they worked on engines of various types, he learned Barry had higher aspirations. Barry asked John, then a practicing psychologist, for assistance with vocational counseling. John agreed. It soon became clear that with all his heart Barry wanted to pursue a career in the medical profession. He had never completed school. After failing the twelfth grade twice, he dropped out to try various jobs, but never found his niche. John found himself faced with a dilemma. The likelihood of a 24-year-old high school dropout gaining access to a university, let alone a medical school, was close to zero. Surely John's professional responsibility was to help him get in touch with "reality" and scale back his ambitions to suit his ability, based on past academic performance. But there was more to Barry than miserable transcripts.

"What intrigued me," John remembers, "was his clear and firm belief in his ability, despite consistent failures. The other option was to encourage Barry to move towards his desired future. I shared my dilemma with him. He decided to seriously begin the journey towards becoming a physician. In spite of all the evidence to the contrary, something inside of me said that Barry was somehow going to accomplish his dream."

Barry returned to school to prepare for university entrance examinations. He even had to get back into a high school uniform. Some of his friends ridiculed him, saying that he had gone crazy, that it would only be a matter of time before he returned to his senses. We've all been in that place before. Whenever we climb out of our everyday rut, others feel threatened! Barry's nay-sayers thought they had proved their point when Barry failed again at the end of that year.

Yet Barry knew he had the ability. He got a job to pay the rent and returned to night school. After another year of study he failed again!

Eventually he failed the exam five times.

Five times, on top of failing the twelfth grade twice! Most would have given up and gone back to motorcycle engines, grateful they still knew which end of a wrench was which. Not Barry.

On his sixth attempt, he passed.

He didn't achieve the required grade to enter pre-medicine, but was granted access to the science faculty, partly due to a "mature student" dispensation. Finally, at 26, Barry Sefton was admitted to an undergraduate program in medical science. He obtained his degree with distinction, received a scholarship to one of the world's most prestigious universities, and today holds a Master's degree in neuro physiology from Oxford University. He still wears his cap backwards, and still fixes engines in his spare time.

65

Self-Wealth

Perseverence

He refused to accept past evidence of shortcomings as failures, and persevered. What is the lesson for us? If Barry can do it, you can too! With determination and self-belief you can achieve your dreams. Think for a moment of all the setbacks Barry faced. Have you faced as many? More? Now experience vicariously his thrill of success each time he shrugged off the setbacks and moved nearer his goal. Imagine vividly that you have just moved a step closer to yours. Enjoy the feeling! Now go take that step!

Here's a mental exercise: Imagine you are trapped in a room. The ceiling appears to be a mirror, with your image reflected back down at you. A part of you wants to get above that ceiling. You wonder about the view from the roof, and imagine it to be exciting, expansive and clear. When you think about this, you get twinges of fear and excitement almost equally mixed. Beyond the ceiling lies the unknown. Maybe this room's not so bad after all: you're warm, and it's familiar. It could grow on you, it's cozy and you feel relaxed. It's what you know.

Just then you notice something. The ceiling is no longer a mirror, but transparent: above it lies an attic filled with all sorts of intriguing shapes and possibilities. You want so much to explore it, and it's within your reach. Your attention is now focused on the attic. All the room is good for is a launching pad.

When we focus on the circumstances in which we find ourselves, it's as if we are back in the confines of that room with the reflecting ceiling. But when we focus on a goal outside ourselves, greater than ourselves, our personal vision enables us to transcend the restrictions of the circumstance. Nelson Mandela proved that in 1964, when he was physically locked into a very dismal room.

Even making it to the jail cell in which he would spend the next 27 years was a kind of victory. When arrested in 1962 he did not know whether he would survive the first night. A number of his colleagues had committed suicide in detention. Others had been executed for treason. This was his room, as described in his book *Long Walk to Freedom:*

> *"I was assigned a cell at the head of the corridor. It overlooked the courtyard and had a small eye-level window, I could walk the length of my cell in three paces. When I lay down, I could feel the wall with my feet and my head grazed the concrete at the other side. The width was about six feet, and the walls were at least two feet thick.... I was forty-six years old, a political prisoner with a life sentence...."*

What sustained Nelson Mandela until he could break free into the attic of a new day for South Africa was his total commitment to freedom for his fellow black South Africans from the bondage of apartheid. His circumstance did not alter his purpose or his commitment.

Nelson Mandela's situation might have been a real ceiling to his life's ambition; at 46 he could have given up. He could have spent his time in that cell dwelling on the injustice of his situation, and emerged a bitter old man ready for revenge. But not only did Mandela refuse to give up his passion, his resolve for change became stronger and more focused. By holding to the vision beyond, he transformed his prison cell from a potential tomb to the office of the country's legitimate president. When he formally took up the presidency of a stricken country, he began to heal it through his own personal example, amazing changes were wrought in incredibly

67

short periods of time—or so it seemed. The truth is that in his mind, he had already assumed that mantle of leadership when he stepped into that cell, and envisioned all the changes to come. It just took the rest of the world a few years to catch up with his vision.

A Vision For Future Opportunities

A goal bigger than yourself enables you to reframe present obstacles into opportunities for the future. It enables you to see through and beyond the ceiling. When Mandela launched his vision quest, any realistic person would have said his odds for achieving his dream were even slimmer than Barry Sefton's. Yet Barry transformed himself—and Mandela transformed a nation! Are your own dreams more ambitious than Barry's? Less ambitious than Mandela's? Somewhere in the middle perhaps? What are *you* waiting for?

John Radford remembers his own bogeyman; it was "sums" in the first grade. It was 1961, and his first teacher, to whom he looked up mightily, was showing the class how to do arithmetic addition. She called it "sums." The students were required to complete a work sheet of problems in simple addition, "but you might as well have asked me to fly to the moon," John remembers.

"I had missed something in her explanation, and could not complete the task. I sat there quite literally paralyzed by fear, not knowing what to do. I never completed one of the sums on that work sheet. She never collected the worksheets and she never asked me for my answers. But the message was firmly in my head:

"John, you are not good enough!

"John, you just can't cut it!

"John, you just are not ready for this!"

It remains one of his most vivid memories of early school years. The feelings of being helpless and out of control associated with this event are as real today as they were almost forty years ago. The context is important. His older brother, James, had begun school the previous year. John had been intrigued by his stories of classroom activities, and could hardly wait for him to come home each day to hear what had happened. At some point the question came up as to whether John would succeed in school. James in his older "wisdom" decided that the best way to find out was to test John with his work sheets.

"I could not complete the work sheets," John remembers. "He eventually pronounced that I would never be ready for school. This was a challenge to any self-respecting five-year-old, so at every opportunity I asked for more tests. I failed each time."

John was somehow sure the real test was still to come. His first teacher would be the one to "officially" decide if he could do the work. Despite that certainty, firmly ensconced in his brain was a message about his inability to perform.

"I was to call upon this message, almost like a tape recording, at many points in my life," John says now. "In most instances I was unaware that I was using this message to judge my capacity to perform. It was so much a part of me that I had integrated it into my subconscious. I had created a ceiling for my performance that had the real potential to block me from even attempting certain challenges, or to withdraw from a challenge prematurely. It wasn't so much because I *feared* failure, but I just *knew* I would fail, so why even attempt it?"

Self-Wealth

John had granted his six-year old brother the status of "authority" figure and that six-year old's pronouncement would cast a long shadow. We live in an uncertain world, and consequently have a strong desire to control our environment and keep ourselves "safe." We work to prevent or slow down change and decrease uncertainty, and avoid circumstances in which we believe ourselves vulnerable. But these attempts are not only futile; they can actually prevent us from dealing with the real, self-limiting issue. Until and unless we believe we can produce desired effects by our actions, we have little incentive to act. This is the essence of what Dr. Albert Bandura describes as *self-efficacy*.

"My first-grade experience provided information that became integrated into my set of beliefs for judging personal performance capabilities," John concludes. "These significant failure experiences are a substantial source of efficacy information because they provide real and compelling evidence as to whether or not one has the ability to succeed."

Building A Resilient Belief

Successes build a resilient belief in one's personal efficacy, while failures undermine such belief, especially when the failures occur before a sense of self-efficacy has been established. We do not place equal value on all our experiences. An experience takes on significant value when you achieve an outcome that was not anticipated; for instance, when you expect to fail but are successful. An experience with a successful outcome becomes a "mastery experience" when your expectancy of failure is overcome by the reality of how you actually performed.

70

Belief is of major significance. John, at five, believed he could do anything. He did not *expect* to fail James' worksheet test.

"I had learned to walk," he says, "one of the most difficult psychomotor skills. Though we all have repeated failures, the belief in our ability to walk results in resilience. But consistent failure, when we intended and expected success, can have the reverse, or negative consequence of lost resilience and confidence."

James' intentions were not malicious. Nor were those of the first grade teacher. The problem was not the intentions of the authority figures, but the flawed conclusions John made on the basis of two significant experiences. He had, without really knowing it, let go of some of his personal control. His self-efficacy was not lowered by intent or by third-party abuse, although abuse is an unfortunate reality for many, with serious negative consequences. John's *perceived* self-efficacy was lowered, and he created his own reflecting ceiling, through ordinary social interaction. Since at the time he did not pay attention to his flawed conclusions, they went unnoticed and unchallenged, and simply became a part of his mental make-up.

Mirrored Ceilings

We all have these mirrored ceilings built into our make-up. Think for a moment: can you recognize some of yours? What limiting effect have they had on your life? What action could you take to make that ceiling transparent—to see through to your renewed sense of self-efficacy?

Why aren't most people more successful? After all, we live in a time when there are so many self-help books and programs available. There are books and manuals to show us methods, procedures and skills to achieve almost anything.

71

Yet in the business world, for instance, we are told that something like 85 percent of new businesses fail in their first year; of the successful minority of enterprises, maybe ten percent of those will still be around after five years. Billions of dollars are spent each year in research, support and training in order to develop "foolproof" business systems that are supposed to enable entrepreneurs to succeed. Something does not add up here. Something is missing!

I believe the answer lies not so much with the competencies, the business systems, the procedures, or the methods, but within individuals themselves. Simply put, successful people succeed—in spite of everything. Our level of motivation, emotional state and actions are based more on what we *believe to be true* than on what is objectively true. There is a whole body of research about beliefs in causative capabilities that has not been adequately conveyed in the literature of self-help. Yet it is in this research, I believe, that the answers for true self-efficacy can be found.

And self-efficacy prepares you to open yourself to Self-Wealth.

If You Believe, It Can Happen

Self-Wealth is more strongly related to a sense of *self-worth* than to a bank balance, or for that matter, any resource to which you have access. Research has shown that people fail to perform optimally even though they know exactly what to do and have the requisite skills. Recently, psychologists have found that successful per-formance has more to do with what you *believe you can do* than with the particular skills at your disposal.

Dr. Bandura, working with others, found that skills can easily be overwhelmed by self-doubts. Even individuals with all the necessary talents make poor use of them, and these shortcomings then further undermine their belief in themselves.

John's academic career in South Africa is a case in point. Self-doubt was his constant companion, despite a Ph.D. in Psychology. Not that he lived each day doubting everything he did. But when really faced with a challenge, John found a part of himself back in that first-grader uniform saying "John you can't do it, you will never be ready, you are not good enough!"

Fighting self-doubt all the way, he completed high school with sufficient academic achievement that granted him entrance into any university in South Africa. Instead he chose to pursue an action-oriented career in the South African Airforce. After eight months, however, he decided that he really did prefer academics; he had so many unanswered questions. In a nearly identical replay of his earlier experiences, an Airforce colonel labeled his decision to leave as evidence of failure and predicted that he would fail also in his academic pursuits. In fact, so convinced was the colonel of his prognosis for failure, he said, "if you ever obtain a university degree, I will personally pay for your tuition!"

Three years later, John was unable to find him to see if he would honor his pledge. It was not all easy sailing. John failed four out of five of the first semester examinations and arrived home declaring that he was "not cut out for it!" The same old message was repeating itself. His parents didn't argue, but reminded him that he had paid for the full year, so why not complete it, "just to see." He did, and went on to his degree.

73

Advantage of Perceived Self-Efficacy

The beliefs we have about our capacity to perform in a new situation are not based only on previous performance. *Perceived* self-efficacy is often a better predictor of success than actual past performance. If efficacy beliefs were solely based on past performance, Barry Sefton would never have persisted. Absent a belief in our own perceived self-efficacy, all of us would be simply pawns of our past, with no capacity to change.

The good news is that development of self-efficacy is a dynamic and ongoing cognitive process, rather than a mechanical audit of past performances. Through life's experiences, and what we think and feel about them, we evolve a structured sense of our "self."

The value we give to new experiences, and how those experiences reshape memory, depends on the nature and strength of the self-beliefs into which we integrate these experiences. Our belief system acts as a filter through which all new incoming information is interpreted. In Barry's case, despite a series of negative experiences over almost a decade, belief in what he perceived to be his innate ability remained intact. The power of pre-set belief in self-efficacy to reduce the negative impact of incongruent performance is strikingly illustrated in Barry's story. Stabilizing self-beliefs serve us well when they are positive. Once a strong sense of efficacy is developed, failure is unlikely to undermine belief in our capabilities. Barry's belief in his ability meant that his personal ceiling was simply a marker to break through to his next challenge rather than a restrictive barrier to limit his performance.

By early adulthood, most of us carry around in our heads a huge database of things we have no intention of trying again. Who wants to bump her head more than once? We pay a heavy price for our fear of failure. It narrows down our options. We are less willing to

74

experiment and explore. We are less likely to risk. Yet the very process of learning involves making mistakes, fumbling, and coming back to try again. And for some of us, it means coming back again, and again, and again.

As John Gardner in his book on *Self Renewal* said, "*If you want to keep on learning, you have to risk failure—all your life. It's as simple as that!*" Without the risk of action, Self-Wealth remains an elusive dream.

CHAPTER 4

Whatever You Think:
Working Towards Balance

"As we let our own light shine, we unconsciously give other people permission to do the same. As we are liberated from our own fear, our presence automatically liberates others."

Marianne Williamson

I define Self-Wealth as the process of achieving balance and serenity, financial freedom and time freedom, optimum mental and physical health, spiritual focus, and meaningful relationships with those we love.

Sounds like a tall order, doesn't it?

We all want happiness. No one wants to be "average." Yet think about the number of people you know who are satisfied with mediocrity. Think about yourself. Are you comfortably settled into mediocrity right now? Notice I did not ask if you are happily settled into it. One of the biggest lies we can tell ourselves is that comfort and happiness amount to the same thing.

At a glance, mediocre lives look safe and comfy. They may even feel that way when we are living them. That's because we have been programmed almost since birth not to rock the boat, not to make waves, not to stir things up—heck, you pick the saying. There are dozens—and they all mean the same thing: don't dare to dream too much; be prepared to settle for what comes your way, or you may lose what little you have.

If you decide to ignore the cautions and "go for it," you often find yourself in a terrific struggle. It's as if you're trying to break earth's gravity and zoom into orbit—in a Piper Cub. The pilot is willing, but the engine just isn't up to it!

That's where Self-Wealth comes in. The principles of Self-Wealth furnish the engine to drive us where we want to go, Self-Wealth principles teach us the *joy of the journey* along the way, and guide us to our destination.

Holistically, from the inside out, Self-Wealth principles give us insight into our own thought processes and show us how to replace negativism with positive affirmations, build self-efficacy and resiliency, and integrate our most deeply desired results into our daily lives.

Limitless Brains Yield Limitless Potential

In 1973, Professor Peter Kouzmich Anokhin of Moscow University concluded a 60-year-long investigation into the nature and scope of the hundreds of billions of cells that compose our wonderful brains.

His conclusion: "No human beings exist who can use all the potential of their brain. This is why we don't accept any pessimistic estimates of the limits of the human brain. It is unlimited."

Unlimited potential? Can this be true? Yes! But if this is true, what's holding us back? Our habits of thinking. Remember the Little Engine That Could? "I think I can, I think I can!"

Every major religious leader and significant philosopher in history has come to the same conclusion concerning human thought. Here's how Buddha phrased it:

"We are what we think. All that we are rises with our thoughts. With our thoughts we make the world."

I would change only one word in his description: "With our thoughts we make *our* world!"

What kind of a world would you like to make?

In this chapter, I want to lay the cornerstone to Self-Wealth: how to harness the potential of our minds by changing the way we think. The tools are these: creative visualization, setting goals, and writing and reciting affirmations. Let's begin to take full advantage of our powerful imagination and intuition. In the Western world, many of us have been taught to disregard these aspects of our intelligence as irrational. This is simply wrong!

Imagination and intuition are the keys to unlocking peak performance.

Re-Educating Your Brain

Have you tried to break a habit lately? If so, you were attempting to re-educate your brain along new thought patterns. Some of the common habits many of us have attempted to break, with varying success, include such things as:

Quit smoking
Stop eating so much chocolate
Get up earlier each day.

Habits are learned behaviors. Anything that can be learned can be unlearned.

We become what we think. Our ability to control what we think about and how we interpret experiences will determine the course of our lives. What happens to us is a direct response to our thoughts.

Habits of thought collect in our mind to become beliefs, and beliefs shape our attitude.

Attitude has more to do with our success than our ability. It's really just that simple.

No matter your present circumstances, you can achieve and acquire anything that falls within the realm of your imagination. I'm not saying you can do this overnight, or that the path won't be marked by difficulties. But I am flatly stating that *the solution is in your mind*, regardless of what some writers have suggested *The Skeptical Inquirer*. I subscribe to that marvelous periodical myself, but sometimes they are simply wrong in their analysis of mind power.

Steps to Re-Educating Your Brain

The steps are simple. First you take responsibility for what you are thinking, or "own" your own thoughts. Then you make a conscious decision to change those thoughts and shape them toward what you really want. Your thoughts will begin to change your habits and your habits will begin to change your beliefs (or vice versa) and altogether, you will find your attitude changing.

Next comes effort and persistence. In many cases we must develop new skill sets to accommodate our new vision. The good news is that your new attitude will free up mental and emotional energy to bring to bear on these skills. As you begin to master whatever skills you have decided are necessary, this will provide positive feedback to your attitude, and the positive cycle will reinforce your improved perception of what is possible.

You will be achieving self-efficacy.

Self-Efficacy

I'll reiterate here that self-efficacy simply means that your own view of yourself is able to shape your own future, and allow you to exercise control over your life. This sense of self-efficacy is vitally important. Many of us want to make changes, but are immobilized. Why? Because we don't have the belief that we can produce results or that we can bounce back from adversity.

We hear a lot about negative spirals these days, where we don't think things will work out, and they don't, and we stop trying, and so of course nothing else works out, which reinforces our negative self-image.

Self-efficacy works the opposite! Self-efficacy is a positive spiral. We build a new strong belief that we can create results. Then we do something—we take action! A positive result feeds back positive support for our belief. A negative result feeds back incentive to try something else, and we act again.

Belief reinforces action, action reinforces belief—and once we are believing and acting as if we have Self-Wealth, we do!

Analyze Your Self-Efficacy

Where do you stand now on personal self-efficacy?

It is my intention to help you assess where you are, and apply the principles I discuss here to increase your self-efficacy. Dr. Albert Bandura outlines the following characteristics of people who possess self-efficacy. As you study the list of traits, think carefully about your present degree of self-efficacy.

How's Your Self-Efficacy?

To what degree do you possess each of these characteristics? The following is not a scientific assessment, but an informal means of getting a sense of your self-efficacy.

Use the following scale:

1 =Never
2=Seldom
3=Occasionally
4=Often
5=Always

☐ I set challenging goals

☐ I sustain strong commitment to my goals

☐ I approach difficult tasks or projects as challenges rather than as threats.

☐ I concentrate on the task at hand, thinking about how to perform successfully rather than dwelling on personal deficiencies, obstacles, or adverse outcomes.

☐ I attribute failures to insufficient effort, remediable lack of knowledge or skill, or unfavorable conditions rather than attribute them to deficient personal abilities.

☐ In the face of adversity, I redouble my efforts rather than slackening off or giving up quickly.

☐ I quickly recover my sense of efficacy after failures or setbacks.

☐ I am receptive to the adoption of new technologies.

☐ In making decisions that carry risks, I make them rather than prolonging the process by collecting redundant information and talking to others largely for self-protective reasons.

☐ I focus in a positive way on the future and enjoy the present, refusing to ruminate about the past or worry continually about the future.

☐ I keep a healthy perspective and do not magnify the severity of possible threats to success.

☐ I let go and do not worry about things that rarely happen.

Add up your scores.

_____

Total Possible Score = 60   My Score = _____

Now ask yourself: What aspects of self-efficacy would you like to improve?

Your next question is probably: Where do I go from here? How do I move to the next level? How do I improve my self-efficacy?

Sources of Self-Efficacy

In his book, *Self-Efficacy*, Dr. Bandura outlines four principal sources of self-efficacy:

- Mental and physical states
- Vicarious experiences
- Mastery experiences
- Social persuasion

Mental & Physical States

Mental and physical states influence how we judge our efficacy. Many theories of depression share a common emphasis to the effect that faulty thinking or ruminant thought is the source of despondency. Depressed thoughts lie to you, and tell you that you are not very efficacious. There is a growing evidence of the impact of our physical well-being on our mental health and vice versa.

Vicarious Experiences

Vicarious experiences are situations in which we gain confidence by seeing someone similar to us succeed and we conclude "If they can do it, I can do it." Many of the stories we share in this book may serve to help you build your self-efficacy vicariously. You must be able to see yourself in the shoes of the person to whom you aspire.

Mastery Experiences

Mastery experiences, in which we are extremely challenged and succeed, stretch our comfort zones to meet the challenge, and we gain confidence.

Social Persuasion

Social persuasion increases our confidence, when we are praised by someone we respect and admire. Their positive assessment of us validates our own sense of self-efficacy. Mentors and coaches are critical.

Our Search For Meaning

Victor Frankl, the famed psychologist who survived the Nazi concentration camps and authored *Man's Search for Meaning* based on what he learned there, concluded that we all search for meaning in our lives, no matter how desperate our circumstances.

A lack of a sense of meaning causes depression. The inability to control ruminative thought (almost obsessively dwelling on past mistakes) can trigger and lengthen bouts of depression.

Perceived self-efficacy is the belief we have about what we can achieve under various circumstances. Our thoughts will determine the degree of effort we exert, our tenacity in the face of obstacles or failures, and our resiliency in bouncing back when reverses occur.

You don't just "imagine" yourself to greatness. Once your imagination has your goal of Self-Wealth firmly in view, you have to do the work to get you there. You have to burn the midnight oil, spend the long hours, gain the new skills, go where you need to, do what it takes—and keep bouncing back when the world hands you setbacks.

It might take you some time. Say the rest of your life.

So what do you plan to be doing with the rest of your life?

Your life will go on, either way, until its end—whether you decide to change, or whether you keep doing the same old thing you've always done, getting what you've always got. It's your choice as to whether the journey is an odyssey of self-discovery, adventure, and Self-Wealth, or that well known, boring, albeit, comfortable rut.

Self-efficacy requires your ongoing investment of time, effort and resources. As you gain self-knowledge, you must integrate it with your skill to make appropriate decisions and take action. Simple hard work is not enough. We all know people who work incredibly hard, but get nowhere: I've done it myself. Just hanging tough doesn't do much for you if you are in the wrong place, repeatedly doing the wrong thing. Who decides if it's the wrong place and the wrong thing? You do. You must take the time to ensure you are on the right road to the right destination, and develop the competencies to travel that road effectively.

"Own" Your Personal Power

Self-efficacy carries with it great responsibilities, risks and repercussions. Risk really is paramount. You must put your self-efficacy to the test, repeatedly. Take the risks. Those with high self-efficacy routinely take risks that those with low self-efficacy avoid. How many of us relinquish decisions and control over our lives to others, just to avoid taking responsibility, or "owning" our own outcomes? Have you been doing that?

Our society is experiencing unprecedented change. Social structures are in flux, technology is intruding into every corner of our lives, and the information age has most of us on information overdose. Chaos and confusion seem the norm within the halls of centralized power today.

In all this turmoil, many of us automatically believe that we have very little control over our lives. A further assumption is that we are incapable of taking control, because we are in a position of powerlessness in relation to the social order in which we find ourselves.

I offer an opportunity to rethink this issue of power from the most fundamental perspective: the power we carry between our ears. Will you *own* this power, or deny it?

If you choose to develop self-efficacy, remember that you will encounter strong resistance from those around you. The strongest resistance, however, will come from your own power-base: your own mind. You will be out of your comfort zone, and your mind will want to help you get back into it. There will be times when the old status quo never looked so appealing and peaceful.

Resistance carries a negative connotation, but it doesn't need to. If you've ever walked into a room full of angry people, you know that resistance is definitely a form of its own energy. You can feel it, humming like a dynamo.

The trick is to recognize your own internal resistance, understand its origin, and redirect its energy in a positive way. This constitutes a formidable challenge in moving towards self-efficacy. We must re-set our comfort zone to avoid subconscious sabotage of our own success.

In her consulting practice, co-author Valerie Bates often focuses on helping leaders of organizations move from dictatorial to facilitative leadership styles. This change is often necessary because the organizations have come to a critical juncture where it is either sink or swim. Increasingly competitive markets require new speed, agility and resourcefulness. Old-fashioned hierarchies are too inflexible.

In order to meet the new challenges, an organization requires a philosophical change from each employee, from the top office to the front line. They must dedicate their hearts, minds and commitment to the success of the organization. There's no time to pause to assign responsibility and power based on hierarchical position or title alone.

Sounds pretty straightforward? Not so. The leaders sometimes resist giving up their authority and control. They fear loss of power and status and don't trust the efficacy of their staff or team. Often, such leaders adopt only portions of the facilitative model, and maintain various aspects of the old hierarchy. Stress levels can escalate and results are less than impressive.

Leaders are not alone in resisting. Staff members resist "owning" any control given them. Sometimes this is because they don't perceive the system to be structured to reward their initiative. Others resist for a more fundamental reason: they don't want to accept responsibility and accountability! They are in their comfort zone as persons without authority.

How about you? Are you prepared to own your power as part of your journey to Self-Wealth?

Imagination Can Equal Reality

Your imagination does not know the difference between an imagined or real event. As you begin to develop your self-efficacy, you need to create a clear picture in your imagination of what you would consider an ideal life. Next use your intuition and analytical thought processes to determine steps to bring your actual reality more into line with your ideal. Then take the steps you envision. If they work congratulate yourself and take more. If they don't work, readjust your thinking, and try again.

The first step is to change what you imagine for yourself. The more clearly and completely you imagine this change, the more readily your activities will change until your experience in the real world comes into alignment with your new self-picture. Your imagination becomes the training tool for your incredibly able brain

88

to develop a whole new way of life. Using your imagination to retrain your brain is the greatest gift you can give yourself.

Why do your activities begin to move toward bringing exterior reality into line with your newly imagined self? Because when you create a strong positive image which does not jibe with external circumstances, you have created something called *cognitive dissonance.* Cognitive dissonance is a term for the emotional state that results from the mind attempting to hold two contradictory beliefs simultaneously.

You have established a very clear picture in your mind about what you truly want. Simultaneously, you are aware of the present reality. The two images do not match. You feel uncomfortable tension. This tension produces energy. You choose how to use this energy. You can let go of your new image, and slide back into your comfort zone. This will dissipate the tension, though there may be a disappointment hangover, since you really liked the new image you created. Or, you can use the tension as a catalyst for action and change, and begin to move your external reality into alignment with your inner image.

Here's a simple example of how this works.

You scheduled a vacation. As the days go by and your scheduled last day on the job approaches, your vacation image becomes clearer and clearer in your mind. Let's just say you're an office worker, and this is the year for that long-dreamed junket to Tahiti. In the last ten days or so before boarding the plane, that office will be less and less satisfying as a place to be every day! Each day, Tahiti sunsets superimpose over the fluorescent lighting. (You never liked that lighting much anyway!) You become more and more dissatisfied with where you are (the office) and more and more anticipatory about where you're going to be (Tahiti). In the last few hours of the last week, that office will seem intolerable! Tahiti is waiting!

That's cognitive dissonance at work. You've already used it in your life, if you've planned a vacation. You already know the technique. All you have to do now is plan the life you want, and get that image just as firmly in your mind as those Tahiti sunsets. Cognitive dissonance will provide you with the energy you need to take action toward Self-Wealth.

Human beings are adaptable. It's how we've survived and taken over the planet. Our natural tendency is to adapt to any situation so that the tension is reduced. That's why the comfort zone is a tough obstacle: we've adapted to daily drudgery as comfortably as our ancestors adapted to daily danger.

But that adaptability can be pressed into service too. Once your vision of the future is strong enough in your subconscious (remember, it can't tell the difference between real and imagined) and you have a strong sense of self-efficacy, you will take action and move toward the vision.

You need to be sure both the vision and your sense of self-efficacy are strong. Both are intrinsic to the process. If either is weak, you may find yourself turning the thermostat back down, adjusting your vision into a more modest one, closer to your present reality. Backing down will reduce cognitive dissonance as surely as moving toward your goal will.

To create your new reality you must set and schedule your goal just as if you already had paid for that Tahiti flight with your credit card. The goal is out there, it is definite, it is scheduled to happen just as surely as that vacation. Just as you pack your bags long before departure day, make preparations for the arrival of your new reality. Anticipate obstacles that may sidetrack or slow you, and have contingency plans to overcome them.

This shows why proper goal setting is so important, and is used by virtually all successful people. Goals, properly established, result in motivation.

To determine whether your goals are properly set and sufficiently challenging, imagine s – t – r – e – t – c – h – i – n –g an elastic band. The top end of the band represents your new vision. The bottom end represents current reality, or your present situation. If you set the vision too far out, you'll stretch the band too tight. It snaps. If you don't set the vision out far enough, then the band is loose, lacks tension and wobbles. It loses its strength either way.

The same principle applies to goal setting. If our goals are too far out there, with no subgoals defined, or—on the other hand—too easy to achieve, either situation acts as a de-motivator. Depressed persons tend to set goals too hard to reach, and then get depressed about failing, which feeds the inability to try again.

Nine Fundamentals of Effective Goal-Setting

Without written targets, and feedback, our energy dissipates. We lose focus, motivation and commitment. Perhaps the most important reason for engaging in goal setting is that we are making a commitment to ourselves to live our lives "on purpose" and stop simply reacting to whatever life throws at us. When we make this sort of commitment to ourselves, and begin to follow through on it, we find balance, provided we have set goals in all the key areas of our lives.

The nine fundamentals of effective goal setting are as follows:

1. Clearly define goals in a specific, written, time-bound manner.

2. Ensure continuous progress by setting new horizons past the last horizon.

3. Begin with the end in mind, focusing on end-results thinking.

4. To create balance, set goals in various areas of your life.

5. Assess honestly where you are today, relative to where you would like to be. The difference between those two factors will create a healthy tension or motivation to move forward.

6. Articulate obstacles and prepare for their arrival.

7. Imprint the goals: write out, visualize and say affirmations.

8. Determine an action plan for moving forward. Include sub-goals so that you take baby steps towards achieving success and building efficacy along the way.

9. Track your performance and adjust your course when necessary.

Achieving Balance

Sometimes we feel that our lives are like a wild horse, galloping out of control. The serenity we so desperately desire will come if we take control of the reins, pull back, and establish balance in our lives. Goal setting is the key to achieving this balance.

There are many techniques that are helpful in goal setting. The most effective technique is to write out your goals. Writing out your goals in each area of your life helps you to clarify and get specific about each goal.

We resist the exercise of writing our goals and values down on paper because the task seems ominous. Actually, it's very simple if we simply let our thoughts flow without analysis and criticism.

Look at all aspects of your life, and design goals for each of the areas in which you wish to improve. If you find yourself feeling overwhelmed, having a hard time visualizing the big picture at first, focus on smaller, short-term goals in the beginning. As you find yourself meeting these goals, you will gain momentum and practice in developing more ambitious ones.

Use the list on the following page to develop goals for eight specific components of your life. Each component has a list of points to think about.

Spend 30 minutes to write out and clarify your goals for each component. Trust yourself. You have the answers in your head right now. Just relax and let your thoughts flow.

Eight Components of a Balanced Life

Inspirational/Spiritual	Nourishment/Physical Health
Finding your sense of Self	Nutrition
Joy	Movement, Exercise
Meaning	Touch, sound, light, silence
Enthusiasm	
God	
Mental Health	**Learning/Education**
Awareness, inner vision	Wonder
Mindfulness	Life as a learning experience
Attitude, Frame of mind	Understanding
Self-talk	Truth, reflection
	Teaching others
Community	**Recreation**
Contribution to others	Spiritual value of work and play
Contribution to earth	Creativity
Multicultural	Relaxation
Nonpolluting	Rejuvenation and refreshment
Loving Relationships	**Career**
Family	Making a difference
Couples, intimacy	Financial Security
Forgiveness, acceptance,	Lifestyle desired
Compassion	Attracting value-driven people to
Trust	your team

Self-Wealth Wheel of Balance

Consider what is most important to your in life. Where do you want to focus your energies in order to balance your life? Use the diagram below and follow the steps below to help you.

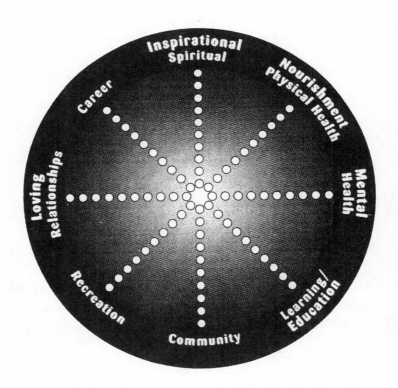

Self-Wealth

1. The spokes of the wheel above represent the eight areas described in more detail in the Components of a Balanced Life chart. Use the points under each component to trigger thoughts. The perimeter or outside of the wheel of balance represents the ideal. Using a red pen, color in a dot along each spoke to represent where you want to be in each of the eight key areas. Using a blue pen, color in a dot on each same spoke to indicate where you see yourself to be at this time.

2. Connect your red dots. This illustrates your desired goals in life in each of the eight key components needed to achieve balance. Connect your blue dots. This illustrates where you are currently in each of the eight key components. Notice the shape of your balance wheel. Is it round or lopsided?

3. Consider the gap between where you would like to be (RED dot), and where you are today (BLUE). Based on this, which of your require the greatest amount of growth? Develop an action plan using the chart on the following page.

Life Balancing Action Plan

Key Area (See Balance Wheel)	Goal	Action (What I will Do)	When
(e.g.) Learning	*Mentor Sally to her full potential*	• *Talk with Sally to Explore* • *Brush up on Mentoring (Read books, take course)* • *Begin mentoring*	*Nov. 11* *Nov. 13 onward* *Dec. 1*

Self-Wealth

S-t-r-e-t-c-h T-e-s-t

Once you have completed the above goal exercise, go back and try the stretch test on each one of your goals to determine whether or not you have created the degree of tension necessary for motivation.

The Power of Intuition

Using analytical, logical intelligence alone will not be enough to experience Self-Wealth in your life. When goals are set, your intuition will come into play in decision making. We need intuitive foresight and vision to anticipate events. We can't accomplish such forecasting through logic alone.

For example, the timing of an endeavor. Any venture needs good timing, but just what *is* good timing? Sometimes logic simply can't answer that question! Fortunately, we have this marvelous intuition to step in where logic is stymied, whether it is the world of finance, business or parenting. Successful business moguls, politicians, and inventors have all had the ability to see the shape of things to come, to foresee opportunities, and to capitalize on them—by using intuition.

Dr. Daniel Cappon, author of *Intuition, Harnessing the Hidden Power of the Mind*, says that our intuition works most effectively when based on our own vast reserves of memory, stored in the subconscious. We often know many things that we don't "know we know" logically, but our experiences and our perceptions of them have been stored way, accessible by intuition in literally the twinkling of an eye. The actual process of intuition is hidden in the unconscious layers of the mind. Stay tuned to your intuition! Your mind will continuously scan the environment for clues to help you access it!

The Power of Affirmations & Visualization

I now want to talk about the advantage of writing out specific instructions to your mind. This can actually bolster your visualization as you meditate by creating a sort of "premature" reality, giving even greater conviction and clarity to your goals. The process is simple, and extraordinarily powerful.

Steps for successful visualizations:

1. Visualize your goal just as you might while meditating.
2. Write it down in your own words, present tense, as if reporting a reality.
3. Read it aloud to yourself.
4. Visualize it again as you read it.
5. Feel it—own the feeling!

Olympic athletes and sports psychologists have known for years that the ability to visualize success and imprint the desired end result into their subconscious is critical to success. The same process will work for us. I use affirmations regularly, as do my co-authors.

Self-Wealth

Through personal experience, we have confirmed that the following formula for writing affirmations is highly effective. The key elements of writing affirmations are:

- include strong emotions
- make them personal
- write them in the present tense
- be sure they are positive

It is very important to keep these affirmations brief, yet specific. Remember the stretch test for setting goals at the correct level? If you've followed our advice and created "goals bigger than yourself," they can be stretched considerably beyond past objectives. Make sure to set your affirmations in the same way—to create dynamic tension for change.

Sample Affirmations

The following are sample affirmations:

"I feel calm, cool and collected (emotional) when dealing (present tense) with irate customers because I (personal) know I am doing my best. (positive, brief, specific)."

"I thrive on excitement, enjoying every minute of my adventure tour to Japan."

"I am kind, firm, fair and consistent with my children because I want them to grow up as happy secure independent adults."

"I enjoy visiting with Mom and Dad every week as they live out their last few years on this earth."

"People listen when I speak because I have something important to say and I speak with conviction."

Application

Look back to the goal setting exercise in this chapter. For each goal and sub-goal write an affirmation (or more than one if warranted). Record them on small 3x5 cards or in your daily journal. Read, visualize, and *feel* them twice each day.

Affirmations and visualizations are very powerful in re-scripting and reprogramming the way we think about ourselves, our potential and our world. Imprinting takes time and persistence. Stay with it. Every time we have a thought, our brains experience resistance. It's like clearing a trail through the woods. The first time is a struggle because we have to fight our way through the heavy growth. Each time we travel the trail, resistance diminishes. Eventually the path is open and well-worn.

Self-Wealth

Our brains will resist our new affirmations of Self-Wealth at first. But our brain is always listening, always ready to adapt. If you keep at it, you will be training your brain in the need for a strong, well-defined mental trail toward Self-Wealth. Don't be surprised if it responds with a superhighway!

CHAPTER 5

Travelling the Road Lighter:

Dump Old Negative Tapes, and Affirm New Positive Ones!

"Truly serene people make the journey of this life with just baggage enough."

Albert Einstein

If you've ever been overnight backpacking you'll know the importance of travelling with a light pack.

"I remember my first three-day hike, at the first stop for lunch those of us who were novices were trying to palm off our heavy food on anyone who would take it. By evening it truly felt as if our backs were killing us. When we broke camp the next morning the garbage cans held an unusual load of equipment, clothing and food that had been discarded in the earnest desire to travel the road lighter," one veteran explains.

Oftentimes our lives seem to be the exact opposite. We start off light, but with each expectation, demand, guilty feelings or buried conflict we hang onto, we add one more item to our backpacks. Rather than shedding the weight so that we can enjoy the journey, we take more on. Material acquisitions can be equally burdensome.

Eventually we spend so much energy supporting the heavy pack that we no longer even notice the beautiful landscape let alone our fellow hikers. Without having planned it that way, we get into a "survival mode" of operation, feeling as if we are ruled by our circumstances and obligations, not realizing we live among a plethora of opportunities. This chapter deals with how we might travel more lightly, so that we have more energy and time to smell the flowers along the way—and see the abundant opportunities around us!

The Clutter of Extra Baggage

Many young children cling to "security blankets" to help them feel better when they encounter new situations. Some years ago it struck me that we all still carry our security blankets—they are just a bit more hidden in our minds. John remembers a few years ago when he noticed that, during operation of the prototype of a new personal development program he created, he would carry a huge document case filled with reference materials. This was his security blanket, helping him feel confident he could answer challenging questions.

This had a thread of logic, except that he had only used this material a grand total of twice in nine years!

That bulging case couldn't possibly hold the kind of information he carried in his head. He finally confronted the obsessive notion, left over from his academic career, that it was absolutely necessary for him to provide documentation for every answer he offered. When he dispensed with this insecurity and began to travel lighter, his chronic back pain miraculously eased. That case had been awfully heavy!

We all carry unnecessary stuff as a means of coping with the symptom of our insecurity rather than its cause. We insist on lugging along a lot of extra baggage from the past—some call them "tapes"—when we start a new chapter in our lives. We kind of ignore the glaring fact that that old baggage—those old tapes--didn't serve us all that well in previous chapters, whether in our career, a relationship, or just dealing with people in general. John shipped and shifted more than a dozen heavy cartons of reference books to four new locations, even across the Atlantic, before he decided to lighten his load and discard all but three of them.

Ever notice how quickly your office, or kitchen, or a drawer, become cluttered with stuff you don't exactly know what to do with when you acquire it? So we hoard it instead of sorting it out and dumping what we know we'll never use. There's another problem that this causes: ever try to find what you do need among all that clutter?

Similarly, our minds are a vast dumping ground for useless and unproductive thoughts. We have vast arrays of memory cells—plenty of room to store all that stuff. The trouble is the mind works like random access memory in a computer, searching through the whole field for bits of information. The more negative and self-defeating thoughts we file away and keep referring to, the more likely they will be right on the surface of our thought processes when we confront an issue that needs our best thinking. We need to sort out what thoughts are valuable and positive, and dump what isn't. The mind just can't hold two mutually contradictory ideas at the same time without conflict, and if we persist in choosing the lighter,

105

conflict, and if we persist in choosing the lighter, brighter thought, our minds will respond with gratitude—just like a backpacker's back—and move us more swiftly and surely toward our destination.

The Weight of Negative Influence

When Blessing Mavundla came into the lives of John and Lorraine in 1986, he was only nine months old. South Africa was in one of its darkest, most violent periods. The civil war had resulted in a weekly death toll that averaged eleven people in their hometown of Pietermaritzburg Umgungundlovu, which in Zulu means: The Place of the Elephant.

John and Lorraine would be Blessing's foster parents for the next six years, and they were faced with a dilemma. On the one hand they had a strong desire to protect this innocent child from the harsh prejudicial society into which he had been born, where skin color determined one's station in life. The messages built in the very structure of the society were that to be "black" was to be less than human. On the other hand, they knew that to protect him could ultimately result in his being unprepared to deal with the tragic reality of this society when he would be forced to confront it someday.

John and Lorraine chose to reinforce Blessing's self-evaluation at every opportunity, and build strong messages within his thought processes about his potential to achieve anything he put his mind to. The plan was to armor him against the shock of individuals who would not look past the color of his skin. In spite of John's and Lorraine's determination to help him build self-efficacy and resilience, his first encounter with the biased external society was traumatic.

"We were shopping together in a toy store," John recounts. "Blessing was a typical four-year-old, lost in the wonder and excitement of the moment, when it was destroyed by a white shop assistant. The assistant grabbed the toy from his little hand and declared she didn't want any more stealing in this store. Furthermore, she didn't want him touching the toys! For an instant we were confused, and then what was happening hit me. For the first time I realized he was the only black child in the store. The other children were playing, without interference, with any of the toys they wished. The shop assistant had just equated the color of his skin with criminal behavior."

Blessing understood the accusation, but obviously was too young to comprehend the underlying prejudice.

"He turned to me," John says, "and with a puzzled, pleading look, asked, 'Why does she think I will steal this? I was just looking!' Inside I was angry, sad, and bitter. It was as if the whole tragedy of the South African situation was conspiring to destroy the soul of this precious child. My first reaction was to lash out with my tongue, and then I remembered our commitment. So I sat down right there on the floor, put him on my lap and, holding back the tears, gave him his first lesson about how not everyone loves us, and that we don't have to accept what everyone tells us.

"I turned to the shop assistant who was glaring down at us and said to Blessing 'Here is a person who wants to hurt you, you don't understand why she wants to hurt you, but that doesn't matter because that is her problem. Do you and I agree that you are not going to accept what she has said to you?' He agreed, we stood up together and left the shop."

This was a very tough experience for young Blessing. But we all have had trying experiences, in which sometimes brutally negative messages are conveyed to us. In travelling the road of life lighter, it is critical that we actively resist these negative inputs. We must consciously reject such negative judgments about us, and refuse to allow them to poison our self-esteem.

We tend to absorb others' comments and attitudes about who we are in an effort to learn about ourselves. We listen for feedback about our effect on other people. This feedback governs how we will respond to them, and then that response garners more feedback, and our learning process continues. Where we sometimes go astray is when we assign too much value and merit to the feedback we receive when it is perceived by us as negative. We can offer even strangers this significant power in our lives. When the individuals offering feedback are truly important to us family members, peers, and authority figures, the effect of negative feedback can be severe. We are constantly shaping and reshaping our perception of who we are. Based on the input and our perception of its worth, we develop expectations of ourselves.

The people we allow to influence our thinking, and therefore our lives, ultimately cause us to add or subtract from our potential. This will directly affect our personal ability to experience Self-Wealth. Don't permit negative or destructive messages to be stuffed into your backpack. Dump this counterproductive mental "stuff" and help others to do the same!

Using Self-talk to Discern Influence

How do we know what messages about ourselves we have internalized as part of us from what we have learned in our relationships? How do we discern those influences that are negative and potentially destructive?

The most effective way is to listen to our "self-talk." Our minds are constantly talking to us, feeding us information about how we should react and feel in a given situation. This process is so automatic that it takes conscious effort to notice the continual internal chatter.

The first step toward unloading the "stuff" is to hold yourself very still. Quiet yourself. Listen to your mind. What is your mind telling you about yourself? Is the constant patter encouraging and supportive, like a winning baseball infield exhorting the pitcher? Or, more likely, is it the unfortunate steady drum roll of doubt and uncertainty? What is your mind telling you that you have learned from all the messages you have accepted as part of yourself? Does your self-talk add or subtract from your sense of self-worth? Do you focus on what will go wrong rather than what is going right? Do you frame almost every interaction and situation in negative terms?

Levels of Self Talk

Just stopping long enough to consciously "hear" this automatic thinking is very important in your journey toward self-worth. It has been called the first level of self-talk. Meditation can help you do this: you learn to be still and yet you are able to become more alert, more aware of yourself. This enables you to hear your thoughts. You must be aware of your automatic thinking before you can begin to reprogram those thoughts!

Next comes the very good news: not only is it desirable to break out of those habits of negative self-talk, it is very possible. Your mind is a marvelous servant; it will do what you tell it to.

Second Level of Self-Talk

The second level of self-talk, when you discern a negative thought pattern, is to tell your mind "Stop!" Just like that: *stop thinking that way.* Your mind will pause obediently, and wait for further instructions. Now take a deep breath and fully realize: you choose what you want to think. You can consciously choose to begin to unload that back-breaking stuff and replace it with lightweight, positive affirmations that will facilitate your journey to Self-Wealth. It won't happen overnight, and it will require some committed effort, but it really is as simple as that.

Unfortunately, when we were young, few of us were taught that we have a choice about what to believe or with whom we should be associated. Much of what we believe about ourselves kind of poured into our minds haphazardly from the words of those around us. Much of it may have been well intentioned, and some of it may not have been. But without the knowledge that we could pick and choose what to accept as part of our self-view, our self-talk is very likely to resemble a patchwork quilt by a beginner.

But as we grow older, we can make deliberate choices about those with whom we choose to associate, and what thoughts we allow to influence us. My co-authors and I long ago made the conscious decision to primarily associate with people who have a positive, constructive approach to life which we find to be amenable to our own positive views. When you think about it, you will realize that life is just too short to do otherwise. Learn to move away from naysayers and doomsayers and be on the lookout for upbeat, positive, supportive and caring people! Surround yourself with those who choose to view you as valuable, and you will find it easier to develop your own sense of self-value. Carefully choose your fellow backpackers on this trail of life!

How to Deal with Negative Comments

When confronted with negative or destructive comments—and we all will be; that's a fact of life—learn to pause and consciously re-frame the situation. Do not just accept the negative "stuff" for your backpack. Here's an example:

Someone is furious with you for not meeting his expectations, and lets you know it in no uncertain terms. From the specific he moves to the general—that is, you have never measured up!

Here's a self-talk response, which re-frames the situation, rather than merely buckling under to the emotional impact of his anger:

"He is angry because I did not meet his expectations, and has said some personally damaging things about my value. He doesn't understand my intentions, and what went wrong. I will apologize to him for my part in the failure, but I will not accept the destructive things he has said about me, because that really is not me. In the future I will check his expectations more carefully. This is a difficult situation, but I have learned something from it."

This puts you in a position of strength, and builds you up rather than denigrating you. Stop saying things to yourself like: "Oh hell, I messed up again? Am I ever going to get it right?"

Fear of negative consequences can lead you to avoid new situations and relationships, resulting in immobility and ineffectual living. We grow by being open to others, not by being closed. We can be open and trusting in new relationships without giving others the right to negatively affect our self-worth. By setting these boundaries, and not permitting negative judgments to cloud our self-perception, we become better partners in every relationship we undertake.

Self-Wealth

My co-author John experienced a loss of trust in a major way when a business partnership fell apart. He says now that he was afraid to even consider another such partnership for some time. He had not dealt with the unresolved pain caused by the failure, and in not doing so, he limited his potential in business and in every area of his life. He had to recognize and deal with his fear that he would not be able to trust the motives of others, and re-frame his experience to the effect that he now is better equipped to discern those motives and deal with them appropriately. Once he could trust himself, he found himself ready to trust others again, and moved on to success.

Valuing Each Moment

In reviewing his own journey to Self-Wealth, John reflects: "If you were to ask me the most significant aspect of my life I would like to change, the answer is simple. I would like to live each moment of my life to its fullest. I would like to spend less time worrying about what is yet to come or regretting what could have been.

"Our lives would be a lot easier," he suggests, "if we could live by treating the present as the first day of the rest of a wonderful life. I am not suggesting that we fall into the western-world trap of believing that the present should be filled with one happy moment after another. To the contrary, some of our finest moments occur in difficult, complex struggles. What I am suggesting is that it is crazy to stop the parade to pick up a penny, yet we do that all the time. How often are we robbing the value of the moment by worrying, feeling guilty, or blaming someone else?"

The Weight of Worry, Guilt and Blame

How quickly does a vision for the future develop into a worry about the future? Examine the logic of this situation. We worry about the future, but we know that most of what we worry about will never happen. Let's say five percent of what we worry about happens. Of this five percent, the probability of influencing the outcome is at most ten percent. This means that we can have an impact on well under one percent of the issues about which we get stressed. More than ninety-nine percent of our worries are truly a waste of our precious time.

M. Scott Peck in his bestseller *The Road Less Traveled and Beyond* has labeled the twentieth century as the Age of Anxiety. With the technological capacity to have world issues spelled out for us in our living rooms, we should feel empowered to influence our societies with positive action. But as the century closed, the opposite occurred.

A world-wide apathy seems to have set in. Hundreds of thousands of people seem unable to respond in any way, or believe they can have any impact at all on the state of affairs. Do you sit in your living room and literally watch the world roll by, and become more and more passive and unresponsive in the face of situations that are often desperate? Over time, many of us learn to be unresponsive to the realities in which we find ourselves. We develop a built-in resistance to dealing with the realities of change. The failure to help others in distress has been described as the "bystander effect."

At the other end of the spectrum lie those who drown themselves in *too much* concern. They have the tendency to take responsibility for people and/or issues that are really outside of our capacity. They worry obsessively about the monkeys riding other people's backs.

113

Those monkeys can weigh just as much as negative thinking! Think for a moment of your own situation: how much are you lugging in your backpack that should be carried by the person with the problem? Is it possible you are burning up your life's energy worrying about something for which there already is abundant worry?

Blame

Another heavy load to bear is blame. Whether we blame others or ourselves for unpleasant happenings, the effort consumed in assigning this blame drains our energy away from the present. Returning our thoughts again and again to some past event, trying to assign and apportion blame, keeps us looking backwards as the present flashes by. To keep ruminating about some past event or relationship is to surrender our accountability for our future. Think about it. Think how restrictive this kind of thought pattern is, how it constrains our freedom.

In order to be free to live in the present and contemplate a future, we must forgive past transgressions—those we committed against ourselves, that were committed against us, or we committed against others. We cannot turn back the clock. We can only make ourselves miserable in the now. Forgiveness is liberating! When you forgive someone for something they have done to you, it not only releases them—it releases you! Forgiveness may be more important to the forgiver than the forgiven! Think how powerful forgiveness of yourself would be! Think of all the weight you could cast from your backpack with such a simple, charitable act as forgiving yourself and others.

Guilt

Guilt and remorse are only valuable to the degree that they create a determination to change the behavior that prompts them. It is important to take responsibility for the consequences of our past actions, and move to correct them where possible. But persistent guilt without a decision to do something about it is nothing less than destructive. Oftentimes guilt about past failures is the handy excuse for our ineffectiveness in the situation in which we presently find ourselves. Worse, it can be an excuse for immobility, for not even trying to develop our full potential.

The following guidelines can help you break from worry and guilt:

1. Think about the things that really trouble you (whether it is some worry or guilt). Consider those things that keep you awake at night while your mind tries to find solutions for them in advance. Use the trigger list below only if your key concerns don't come to mind easily.

    Children
    Key close relationships
    Your Health
    Finances
    Accidents
    Disturbing situations
    Events

2. Do any of these concerns belong to someone else? If yes, discard them by drawing a line through them. Next to each of the cancelled concerns, write the names of the persons to whom they rightfully belong.

3. When you have determined which concerns truly belong to you, write your three top guilt or worry issues down on a sheet of paper. Examine what effect your concern will have, if any, on the outcome of those concerns. Write your thoughts next to each one.

4. If you find a concern that you can affect, write down what you need to do now to change the predicted outcome. For those concerns over which you can have no impact, take your pen or pencil and cross them out.

5. Now create a positive affirmation about concerns. For example: "I choose to only trouble myself over those matters which I can change. I continually check my self-talk to determine whether I am still worrying about issues on which I have no impact."

Valuing Failure as Success

We live a world where we want things to happen instantly. The thing we prefer to happen most instantly is gratification. We want things to occur for us without too much effort, and in the absolute minimum period of time. By today's standards, anything less is considered failure. With this attitude, it is no wonder that attempts at self-improvement tend to show a low success rate.

Self-improvement is not an overnight thing. Self-Wealth is an on-going commitment that you must pursue with passion for the entire course of your life. With this commitment must come the knowledge that many times you are going to fall short of your plan, and many times you are going to be completely off course. You must acknowledge and accept those things, and determine that when you fall short, you will accept the lesson and move on; and when you are off course, you will make a mid-course correction and keep moving.

Fly on Autopilot

It is an interesting navigational phenomenon that when an aircraft locks on to a directional beacon under its automatic pilot, it travels approximately 90 percent of its flight in error.

Each time the aircraft strays off the beacon, its aircraft guidance system corrects for the error and moves it back on course. Winds aloft, barometric pressure, many things can influence the flight of the aircraft. Thus the entire flight path is a series of errors, continually corrected in mid-course as the journey progresses. Paragliding is 99% going the wrong direction, yet an experienced pilot can land on a quarter inch ribbon in a one mile square field!

What does this teach us? Don't worry about being off course! Instead, learn how and when to make your mid-course corrections. Develop confidence that the journey is generally proceeding as it should, and keep alert for the necessary corrections. Every failure we experience then becomes part of our success. Failures are indicators that we are moving, and learning as we move.

Carrying this thought out to its logical conclusion, it is virtually impossible to make a wrong decision with respect to our own development, once we have determined our goals and destination. We will only go wrong if we let the nose of our craft stray off-course without moving to correct it at once as soon as we see that we are drifting.

In his studies, Dr. Bandura found that this ability to make mid-course corrections is critical to building resilience. Our perception of our own ability to perform is increased and made more enduring every time we overcome an obstacle and persevere towards a challenging goal.

Goals Must be Challenging

The goal must be challenging. If we experience success with few failures and little effort, we come to expect this every time. This reinforces the societal expectation of instant results. That can become a problem when we suddenly run into turbulence or severe obstacles, because such events following an easy run could lead to us into becoming easily discouraged. It is imperative to view failure as part of our success path. By viewing reverses in this light, they become just another confirmation of our forward progress.

You will know you have learned this lesson when, in the course of your own quest for Self-Wealth, you begin to see each obstacle and reverse as valuable information en route to your objective, rather than a demoralizing defeat.

Building resilience is not easy; at times it can be painful. But in order to grow, and move toward experiencing Self-Wealth in your life, you must learn to accept pain as part of the learning experience. We've all done this in our lives, as early as when we learned to walk by banging into things and toppling over repeatedly.

Let me give you a simple example of resiliency. John's daughter is learning to skate. The symbolism of the bruises on her young legs is very important to her. She is learning far more than the skill of skating. She is learning a basic lesson of life. The pain of each of her falls is very real at the moment of impact. Those impacts are what result in the bruises she wears so proudly. And why is she so proud of the bruises that bear mute testimony to her falls and her pain? Because as she focuses on her goal of graceful skating, it is not the pain she remembers but the joy of success. Each time she skates, she skates a little better. Her bruises are purple badges of courage and perseverance.

But what if she attributed her bruises to her lack of physical ability? Well, she would look at them and develop reasons not to go to the next skating lesson. They're too sore, they need time to heal; maybe it's time to take a break from trying to learn to skate. She would be on her way to giving up more readily in the face of difficulty. Given that thought process, each of her bruises would be symbolic of one more failure, more unwanted stuff in her child-size backpack.

But she's got the right attitude. And attitude is everything, when it comes to resiliency. What activity or goal has bruised you lately? How are you processing that information? Are you approaching it like John's daughter? She credits her increasing skill on the skates to her personal capability. She credits her failures ("I just need to try that again!") to insufficient effort. When she examines her bruised legs at bath time, she is proud of them. They have become trophies of her success journey.

Look at those bruises of your own. You earned them! Now get back on your personal set of skates, whatever that might be—and go for it again!

CHAPTER 6

You are Fail-Safe:

Resiliency is the Key

"Being defeated is often a temporary condition. Giving up is what makes it permanent."

Marlene Suvant

Think it's too late to experience Self-Wealth in your life? Do you wish you had been encouraged to "go for it" ten, twenty, even thirty years ago? It's never too late! History is replete with examples of women and men who shrugged off destructive or mediocre lives, developed resiliency and an unrelenting desire to better themselves, and ultimately triumphed.

From Playboy to Sainthood

Let's consider this guy, Augie. He was a playboy among playboys; in an age when excesses were common, he was notorious. His drinking buddies must have been bewildered when he first refused a drink and then stopped chasing (and catching) women. He had been the life of every party, the stud of every encounter, for twenty besotted years.

Then, abruptly, Augie left town. He began a self-imposed exile of introspection. He read, he wrote. But his change did not come easily. On numerous occasions the siren song of wine and women lured him back to his former haunts. His friends and lovers would welcome him back with open arms and open bottles. It would have been easy to surrender to his life's former pattern again.

That's where resiliency came into play. He never surrendered. Each time he slipped back into old ways, he would again make the decision to cork the bottle and turn his back on the beguiling flesh.

By the time he made his decision stick, he only had ten years to live. But he settled flawlessly into his new contemplative life. In that decade, he authored ethical codes and treatises on morality that have been for centuries, and remain, a daily inspiration to millions of people on every continent. He is known today as Saint Augustine, one of the pillars of philosophical and religious thinking.

Comments From the Peanut Gallery

Resiliency is the ability to persevere toward your objective through life's inevitable setbacks, without becoming sidetracked or

121

immobilized by condemnation, ridicule or even well-meaning advice from bystanders. When you commit to a life based on the principles of Self-Wealth, you climb out of the spectator seats and plunge into the center of life's arena.

One problem you will encounter is that other spectators, particularly family and friends, will be alarmed to see you vault onto the field. Some will fear for your safety out there; others will find their own comfort zone—in which until now you have been a settled part—disturbed.

Those close to you will cheer if you score early successes out on the field. But when setbacks occur, or you go down hard, they will join in urging you back to the sidelines—again, out of fear for your well-being, or to restore their own sense of comfort, or more likely a combination of both. You gave it your best shot, you may be told; now quit while you're behind. Or you may hear the more hurtful "I told you so."

Those who succeed over and over, going on to be remembered with respect long after their particular generation has gone, are those who stay on the field and continuing playing on, play their best, despite such well-meaning reactions.

Beyond family members and friends sit those who have elected to spend their lives on the sidelines. They slurp beer and gobble hotdogs, participating as Monday-morning quarterbacks every play of the game. They will often have very harsh opinions of your performance on the field. Your resiliency must include the ability to play on, play hard, keep your eye on the ball, without regard to these armchair generals. Trying to maintain the proper impression to please everyone requires entirely too much energy. We call this attempt to please "impression management." In the final analysis, crowd applause is of little value in achieving Self-Wealth. The moment you step boldly onto life's real playing field, many of those left behind are forced to deal with a certain envy that never seems to fully go away. You must develop a resiliency that bounces back from sideline sniping based in this envy. Impression management is the pathway to self-imposed mediocrity!

Resliency: Brew Your Own Chicken Soup

Walt Disney was stone-broke when he created perhaps the best-known cartoon character in the world, inspired by a mouse. He declared bankruptcy two times before launching Disneyland. Mother Theresa was expelled from her convent four times for what were then considered immoral antics before establishing more hospitals in indigent villages than any other human being in history. Rocky Blier scored a winning Super Bowl touchdown after recovering from Vietnam injuries which orthopedic surgeons insisted would prevent him from ever running again.

We could fill this whole book with stories of resilience, but that's not our goal. If you need more inspiration, there are probably now Chicken Soup books for every soul that ever existed, and probably for some that haven't. A lot of those books are fun and inspiring to read. My suggestion to you, the student of Self-Wealth, is this: work on your own inspiring story. Brew your own chicken soup.

And should you decide to do that, I encourage you to include two key ingredients in your "stock" for the chicken soup pot as you progress towards experiencing Self-Wealth. Each of these ingredients will enhance your resiliency many-fold, and if applied consistently will bring astonishing results into your life. If you prefer, rather than the cooking metaphor, you might think of these two ingredients as essential tools for your Self-Wealth tool chest.

The First Tool: "This is called..."

"TIC" is the first tool I want to share. The initials stand for "this is called..." Here's an example.

Bill is a brand-new life insurance salesman. He's been trained to "pitch" friends and family. He understands his products, and has been taught the answers to most predictable objections. Bill optimistically calls his best friend, Steve, and uses his finest canned approach.

Steve turns Bill down cold. Essentially hangs up on him.

Bill can now experience a number of negative emotions: his friend rejected him; his sales pitch is lousy; if he can't sell his best friend he's never going to make a sale, etc.

But here's the way to deal with Bill's problem:

First, remove yourself personally from the disappointing event with the following statement:

"This is called a friend turning down another friend who wishes to sell him life insurance..."

Using "TIC" self-talk, Bill removes emotion from the situation, and becomes an objective observer. He defines the situation accurately, without emotional baggage.

Next, he finishes his self-talk with positive instruction:

"...but that's okay. Selling is a numbers game. Every time someone says 'no' I am that much closer to a 'yes.'" And this is more than a cliché, it is simply a fact. Approach enough people and eventually you will make a sale.

Now, the process of detachment, definition and positive reinforcement may sound like Bill is rationalizing his demoralizing rejection by a friend. Yes, he is. It is exactly that—he is defining the situation rationally. This is the rational management of failure, especially in the earliest stages of your new endeavor, so that the setback becomes educational rather than emotionally discouraging. Applied consistently, TIC will immeasurably enhance your sense of resiliency and eagerness to confront the next challenge, and the next, and the next, etc.

As you find yourself adopting TIC to your challenges on a daily basis, you will invoke the process of experiencing Self-Wealth. Detached observation is a very powerful tool.

In 1979, I delivered a sermon at Christ Church Unity in Springfield, MO, entitled "The Christian T.I.C." The gist of my sermon was this resiliency process. For the purposes of the church-going audience, I introduced the concept of "forgiveness" into the equation. In the foregoing example, Bill's internal dialogue would have been more along these lines:

"This is called a dear friend rejecting a concept. But I will forgive that friend because not everyone needs or wants life insurance."

To this day, according to the church secretary, cassette tapes of that simple sermon are still the most-requested audio from a Sunday service, fully two decades after I spoke. Here's a recent letter requesting this speech:

"...I am writing to request another ten tapes of the great sermon on the Christian T.I.C. system. Using that simple approach in 1982, I set a national sales record for a large Mutual Life Insurance Company and this year is my fifth invitation to serve as a keynote speaker at the Million Dollar Roundtable proceedings in New York. I like to always have several tapes of the sermon available to hand out to leaders who ask me the key to my success...."

Needless to say, I am very proud that my sermon has been sought by so many. What made it so popular? I am convinced it was—and is—the recognition by people of how effective TIC would be in their own life situations.

TIC works! It builds strong resiliency. Put this method to work for you right away.

The Second Tool: "Solicited Critique Model"

Everything we attempt has the possibility of success or failure. Success is often its own reward. But what of failure? We can let failure be its own punishment, which perhaps douses our spirit or makes us reluctant to try again. Or we can view every failure as an opportunity to gather information.

My second resiliency tool for your success and Self-Wealth is what I call the "solicited critique model." This tool is both provocative and, I believe, unique to Self-Wealth.

Before I get into the specifics of solicited critique, let me offer a bit of advice about unsolicited criticism: I think we all wonder about the motives of those who offer us unsolicited negative criticism. When this comes your way, no matter how painful, listen closely, and pay no attention to any perceived motive. Even if the critic's motive is less than pure, the criticism may offer us information of value. Criticism, in any form, for any reason, can be quite educational if we pay attention to the critique, not the imagined motive.

126

Now let's look at the "solicited critique model," where you actually seek information about possible shortcomings you may need to overcome.

I think negative criticism is such a valuable part of the journey to Self-Wealth that I urge you to use our technique to draw the negative information out of those who have, until now, been silent about your performance. Before you think I am contradicting all my other points about focusing on the positive, hear me out.

Regardless of your daily calling in life, you will face interactions with others whose opinions are important to you. This, of course, applies most obviously to entrepreneurs attempting to build a business from scratch, and to sales personnel who are trying to move products. But it also applies if you are planning to build a house and need to get your permits from a reluctant municipal authority. It applies if you want your teenager to seriously consider the consequences of actions his or her peers are pressuring them to take. From business to personal relationships, your interactions with others will determine what you receive from them. You may think you've done the best presentation of your views or wares that you possibly could—but what do the people who don't agree with you truly think?

Employing the Solicited Critique Model

For the sake of simplicity, let's use the model this time in a sales situation, as we did the TIC model.

The first step is simple: keep a list of those people who do not buy what you're trying to sell or promote. They could be life-insurance prospects, network marketing customers, or bank presidents who reject a software-tracking system. Let's go with the software-tracking example.

Bill owns XYZ Software Company. His tracking system is the very finest available for the banking industry. Each day Bill prepares a list of bank presidents as his prospects. He obtains interviews with an average of four per day and that requires 40 approaches. Of the ones who agree to an interview, one out of 10 actually becomes a customer. Because the software package is a "big ticket sale," Bill needs only obtain one customer a month to remain highly profitable. The natural tendency in a situation like this is to keep finding new prospects and calling them, day after day, and putting aside any thought of those who turned him down.

But under the solicited critique model, Bill would put aside an hour each day specifically to call back those bankers who had either refused him an interview or failed to buy after he made his pitch: His next approach would go something like this.

"Hello again, Steve, this is Bill from XYZ Corp. We talked briefly about my software tracking system last week. I wanted to thank you again for giving me some of your time then. I'll even be more brief this morning. I am asking you for your honest evaluation of my sales approach. What can I do to improve my presentation to bank presidents of your stature? Please be blunt: what did I do or say that was not effective? I would be very grateful if you could identify shortcomings that I have overlooked."

Often Bill will find that most people will not be blunt, but courteous, pointing things out for Bill to consider. They might say his presentation was poor, or they didn't have the authority to make such a purchase, or that the bank already has an effective system. But candor often evokes candor in return. They may recall the presentation, and they may just tell Bill specifically what he said or didn't say that turned them off. Remember: No matter how well you think you do, how poorly these failed prospects think you did is crucial information.

No one can offer more valuable feedback to you than the person who chose not to purchase what you were trying to sell or accept what you were trying to impart.

You will already have known from your marketing research that the company you pitched is a qualified lead—that is, they've got the money to afford your product, and they use such products or need to. When your sales approach is declined, the odds are very strong that it was due to some deficiency in your approach. Constructive criticism from the prospect that "got away" is an invaluable learning experience.

Now consider this: in spite of the value of such solicited criticism, a recent survey in *Success* magazine disclosed that less than one percent of all entrepreneurs seek constructive criticism from those who reject their pitches.

As a serious student of Self-Wealth, you should begin to immediately implement this strategy.

When you do, you effectively lift yourself above the competition, simply because most professionals never seek constructive feedback from those who reject their offers.

Remember the Self-Wealth model emphasizes that resilience leads to success, and resilience is developed through perseverance.

You will tend to persevere when you enjoy recognition and rewards along the way. This model allows you to convert failed attempts into beneficial information gathering. When you receive the information that lets you modify your approach, you have created a modicum of success out of what before were merely failures. At the very least what you will earn from this model is enhanced respect from those you contact. Who can resist a person dedicated to self-improvement?

Getting Personal

Each time you appropriate constructive criticism into your modified approach, your opportunity for success is dramatically improved. While I used business situations for ease of illustration, I think you can see how this technique will pay big dividends in personal relationships as well.

To review, both the TIC system and the "solicited critique model" are both non-invasive but practical tools to use in your quest for Self-Wealth. Those who do employ these tools often experience dramatic improvements in relatively short order. Try them yourself, right away. See if you don't achieve unexpected, dynamic results.

Application

Think about a recent disappointing situation in which the TIC System might work for you. Write down what happened. Write, "this is called..." and re-frame the situation objectively.

Solicit constructive criticism about your performance from a family member, a friend, a colleague, a client or customer. Listen openly and learn from the feedback.

CHAPTER 7

For All You're Worth:

Rediscover the Value of Self

"Happiness cannot be traveled to, owned, earned, worn or consumed. Happiness is the spiritual experience of living every minute with love, grace and gratitude."

Dennis Waitley

Without a strong sense of self-worth, it will be difficult to build the self-efficacy required to achieve Self-Wealth. You should take the time to explore what you think you are worth now. This is the foundation for moving forward.

To have a strong sense of self worth you must like yourself. You must know yourself, including your not-so-perfect traits.

Acquiring self-knowledge and assigning self-worth is a complex topic worthy of its own book, and many books have been written on the subject. One of the most influential thinkers in this area is Carl Gustav Jung, a contemporary of Freud's whose works created a whole separate school of psychological thought.

Jung's Personality Model

Jung developed a model of our personalities that describes six layers of self-awareness, contained in a sphere representing "self." He calls these layers persona, and proposed that these six individual personalities must live in harmony and balance in a healthy mind. Unhealthy minds lack this balance, because the inner persona are sometimes violently opposed to each other, and the over-arching "self" is unable to hold them together.

Jung's model has withstood the test of time, and helps us understand the internal contradictions each of us faces. Let's take a look at three of the six layers: the outer layer, hidden shadow layer, and the core, or SELF.

Another way to describe these layers is the *public self*, the *personal self* and the *private self.*

The outer layer or persona, the public self, is the one we allow others to see. Our "mask" is often useful in a world where not everyone has our best interests in mind, and we wish to protect our heart, our emotions. The public world knows only this outer layer, which we employ in an effort to impress others with our presence and our credentials.

Who Are You?

Facing someone from the outside world who demands a look beneath the mask can be disconcerting. While studying conflict resolution, my colleague and co-author Valerie Bates met a young man named Brian who, after a quick introduction, looked her straight in the eyes and demanded: "So, tell me, Valerie, who ARE you?"

Valerie knew that Brian was asking her who REALLY lurked beneath the brisk demeanor, business suit and briefcase. She was taken aback, and since she is rather reserved, she responded from her outer layer: "I am a mother, wife and I've been a consultant for the last eight years."

Brian's simple question lingered after the encounter. Valerie was at the time moving from one career field into another, a time for introspection. Brian's question reverberated in her brain: "Hmmm, *WHO AM I?* Does the outside match the inside?"

The outer layer is useful, provided it is flexible, and serves as a soft protector rather than a hard shell or impermeable suit of armor designed to distance us from intimacy. If the public self is too distanced from our core self, a hard shell can become so heavy that it drains our energy. Think about your own situation. How closely does your exterior reflect what is at the core of your being?

Our Shadow Side

The next layer to consider in our search for self-awareness is our *shadow* side, so-called because it has been buried deep within us, not because it is necessarily sinister. We have submerged it in response to social and cultural pressures that teach us that certain facets of our nature are inappropriate, wrong, distasteful or evil. We fear exposing them may result in our rejection. For some of us, hiding our shadow becomes a prime focus of our energy. Many around us sense something amiss. The strain of hiding this part of ourselves is terrific. One of the most liberating acts as we move toward self-knowledge is to shake hands with our shadow; come to terms with this part of us, and not deny it.

Our SELF

The very central layer or integrating force for all the layers of persona is the SELF. This private self also has been called the anima, the soul, the "ghost" in the clockwork machine of the brain. At this core, in our innermost self, is where we connect to every other human being. The SELF is the place where we are joined in sameness. The SELF has nothing to prove; it's the place where we know who we are or we have a feeling of "being home." It is bathed in beliefs. Carl Jung believed that this SELF is whole and in fact, this SELF is love. To be healthy, a person's outer persona and shadow persona must not be too out of synch with the SELF, and the healthy person is aware of the differences that exist, and allows for them.

In the application section of this chapter you will have an opportunity to assess your own personality against Jung's three layers of being. Use it to explore your personality further and gain insight and motivation to change if necessary.

Life offers plenty of opportunities for self-awareness when it knocks us off our feet, forcing us to stop and search for answers. But we don't have to wait for a jolting experience to become more self-aware. We can today move out of that reactive attitude to a pro-active mode by applying the following methods, and get to know ourselves better on our own terms.

Self-Wealth

Here are nine ways to approach this undertaking:

- Layer Upon Layer Upon Layer
- Rise and Shine Morning Pages
- Nature as your Psychologist
- Prayer and Meditation
- Mind Mapping
- Third Party Neutral
- Champion Feedback
- Assessment Tools
- Hearts, Values, Actions!

Layer Upon Layer Upon Layer

Take a look at yourself and your "layers." What words, attributes, roles, characteristics describe you? Make use of the diagram that follows or create your own diagram on a separate sheet of paper. Then write surface connections in the outer layer or the persona. For example, you might write your profession in the outer layer if you do not connect deeply with your profession. However, if it represents yourself, you might write it closer to SELF. Once you have completed the exercise for yourself, you may wish to go through the same exercise again, but this time write the description of someone (or of several others) you love. At the right moment discuss it with them.

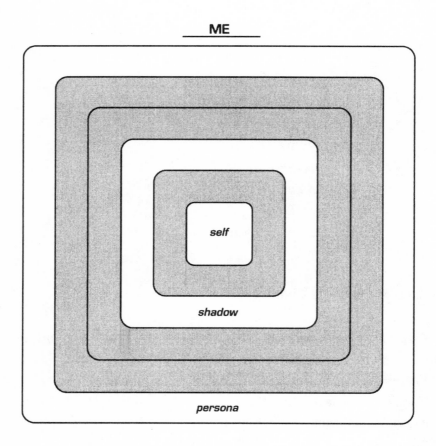

For years Valerie has taught process-facilitation skills programs to help people in the corporate world and public service sector lead organizations, communities, and teams in planning their futures, developing strategies and making effective decisions.

Self-Wealth

Self-awareness studies were added to enhance the outcome of the program. Once facilitators increased their self-awareness and developed a positive sense of self-worth, they were better able to master basic values such as treating everyone with dignity, admitting mistakes, remaining as objective as possible, and refusing to facilitate any endeavor which was merely an exercise in manipulation. The effectiveness of the techniques they acquired improved because they were much clearer about who they were and what their own worth was.

"Rise and Shine Morning Pages"

There's nothing better for self-awareness than getting up first thing in the morning and writing down the first things that occur to you. Recording your thoughts in a journal, or *journaling*, up to three pages each day releases tension and anxiety, and opens your mind. Your writing might include how you are feeling, what you are planning, your concerns and hopes for yourself and others, or your insights into yourself and others.

Your writing does not have to be sophisticated. You can write any thought that comes to your head like, "Do I need to stop at the store today? Didn't I just do that two days ago? Why didn't George return my call? I think I'll go to the gym today." As the words flow, amazing insights will surface. The connection between the newly awakened brain and the hand holding the pen or pencil is intimate and direct. Your own words will often surprise you. Start right away. That's up to three *handwritten* pages each morning. One caveat: do *not* share these pages with anyone else. These words are yours alone in your ongoing discovery of self-awareness.

Nature As Your Psychologist

A world-class psychologist is right out your front door: all outdoors and Mother Nature await your personal retreat for introspection and meditation. A favorite spot surrounded by nature is ideal, provided humans are scarce and birds plentiful. We all enjoy different retreat spots. Some crave the ocean, others enjoy sitting on a hill overlooking a small tranquil lake, and still others love the desert. Seek your own spot that resonates with you. Schedule time there as faithfully as you would with a paid analyst! This is your personal time for *aloneness.* You need it to rejuvenate or re-create regularly, and your world-class therapist is quietly waiting for your visit.

You must find a balance between action and reflection. Most of us are so busy each day that we take no time to listen to messages from our layers or parts of ourselves. Busy-ness is our enemy. Motion often is mistaken for progress. Learn to regularly pause, spend time alone and cherish that time as an opportunity to get to know yourself.

During such retreats, simple questions such as those following remind us of the beauty in our lives, our vision for the future, and can fortify us against those things that we find distasteful or destructive. Take your journal with you, and answer the following questions, as you pause and reflect:

- What do I like/love about my life?
- What would I like to add to it?
- What do I absolutely NOT want in my life? *Travel, Retirement, Security*
- What are my life goals? Short term? Long term?

Volunteering

If you do not have access to a special place, find one in your imagination. Sit in front of a sunny (or rainy) window and close your eyes. Travel in your mind to your favorite spot; perhaps one you knew as a child or teenager. Sense the clean air, the sounds of nature, the wind on your face. Relax and imagine you are there. Now ask yourself the questions, and listen to your answers. Write them in your journal. Listen and learn.

Prayer or Meditation

Prayer provides us with a peace that is not of this world and offers a chance to get to know our true selves. It helps us release anger, find forgiveness, achieve intimacy and mend relationships. Through prayer we create a better inner life for ourselves and for those we love. For those uncomfortable with personalizing a supreme being or God, meditation is highly effective at increasing self-awareness by shutting off the internal dialogue.

In our daily grind, we repeat the same internal "self-talk" over and over; and make the same choices consistently. When we call for silence in order to still this internal monologue, we open ourselves to possibilities. Whether we pray or meditate, the silence allows for reflection and personal growth.

Mind Mapping

We all have an imagination. We do not have to be artists to be creative, but we all need to express ourselves in a creative fashion regularly to tap into areas of ourselves that linear thought processes cannot access.

Mind Mapping is one creative process that uses a full range of cortical skills on both sides of our remarkable brains, and therefore offers a more comprehensive access to ourselves than through linear, or "outlining" methods of expression. Tony Buzan, author of *The Mind Map Book*, recommends mind mapping as a process for accelerating self-analysis. A Mind Map Self Analysis encourages greater awareness of our needs, desires and visions for our lives.

A mind map starts with a central point in the middle of a page. It can be a word, drawing or image. From this center, lines radiate 360 degrees to each new thought or concept triggered by the process. The radiating structure of a mind map reflects the natural architecture of the brain, and helps retrieve widely disparate and seemingly unconnected bits of data in a rapid fashion. Let the thoughts and words flow onto the page.

The result will be a snap shot of what's going on inside your brain. You then can link key concepts, shaping a clear concise picture or map of all relevant points. By incorporating the use of shapes, colors, and dimensions as visual stimuli, Mind Mapping allows us to make the best use of all our considerable mental resources. My co-authors and I have used Mind Mapping not only for increasing self-awareness, but also for a variety of explorations, including writing this book.

Mind Mapping Exercise

Below is a step by step explanation of how to use Mind-Mapping.

Step 1: *Prepare your environment.* Create a calm environment and make yourself comfortable. Relax. Make sure you have plenty of colored pens with you. Study the following sample mind map.

Sample Mind Map

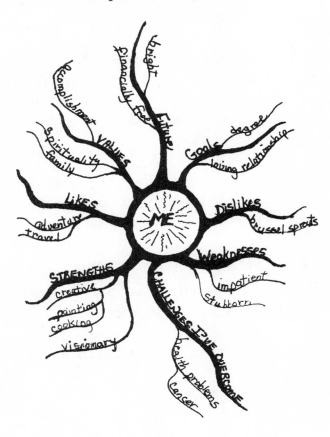

Step 2: *Draw a central image.* In the middle of your page, draw a multi-colored central image of yourself.

Step 3: *Draw a Quick Burst Mind Map.* Begin drawing a Mind Map quickly, allowing yourself random and spontaneous thoughts like "bursts" of creativity. Draw curved lines radiating from the center picture of yourself and write your ideas along the lines, making connections where possible. Allow yourself to free flow thoughts. Work randomly.

Write any attribute or insight you have about yourself. Link ideas to each main "artery" where appropriate. Keep adding to the description any trait of yourself that comes to mind. Add ideas, facts, and emotions about your past, present or future.

Use plenty of colors. Wherever possible draw a picture to connote your idea rather than using words, although words will work as well.

Step 4: *Reconstruction.* Redraw your mind map, taking the time to add color and creativity. Look for connections and insights. Select primary branches such as:

Personal History – past, present and future
Strengths
Weaknesses/Problems
Likes and Dislikes

- Long Term Goals
- Family
- Friends
- Achievements
- Interests

Step 5: *Insights.* Ask yourself what insights you have into who you are, your values, vision of the future. Consider how your mindmap relates to the Wheel of Balance and the Balance Plan you completed in an earlier chapter.

Third Party Neutral

When we consider all these facets of our personality, it is no wonder we experience internal conflict. How do we ensure that all these parts of our personality work together in harmony? How do we understand ourselves and others better? We employ "Third Party Neutral." The term and technique were developed by The Canadian Institute for Conflict Resolution.

Step outside yourself and view both your thoughts and the behavior of other people from the external position as a Third Party Neutral. You are fully present to your thoughts, listening without judgment, defensiveness, excuses, impatience, or preconception. In this safe space, you actually tell yourself the truth, the real truth and nothing but the truth.

You remain as neutral as possible, and open to every one of your perspectives about yourself. Your goal is to solve your problems without causing harm to yourself or anyone else. You are very

143

attentive to your feelings of pain, angst, anger, joy or sorrow. You are more interested in resolution and long-term success than a short-term, narrow minded "win." You insist on ground rules that include no name-calling, and that everyone has a chance to tell their side of the story without interruption. Consider how often we call ourselves names and shut out hearing different internal perspectives.

Third Party Neutral Application

After you have learned to assume a Third Party Neutral role within yourself, you can assume that role when dealing with others. How does this translate into a real world application? Here's a possible scenario:

One day, your sixteen year old daughter says, very matter of fact, "Mom and Dad, I know how hard this might be for you to understand, but I'm moving back to the island where we lived for three years. I've made all the necessary arrangements. I have a part-time job and I can live with my best friend's family. I love you, but I'm not happy here. The most important thing in the world to me is spending my last year in high school with my good friends and graduating with them. After all, you moved me out of my comfort zone at a very awkward time last year when we moved away from the island. Oh, and by the way, I'll leave on the weekend. I'm all packed and ready to go."

You pause, pick your brain up off the floor and resist the temptation of the "name and blame game." You take a deep breath, call time-out, and leave the room to gain composure. You step into Third Party Neutral from two perspectives: one for yourself, to find what you are really feeling, and the other from your daughter's point of view.

144

You ask yourself how to handle this situation so that no one is hurt and your long-term relationship remains healthy. What is best for her? What is behind your concern? You answer those questions quietly to yourself and with candor. You are honest about how you are feeling and why you feel this way. You commit to listening to her side of the story and empathizing with her. You're open to exploring options.

You walk back into the family room as a Third Party Neutral, knowing that you can work this out and stay open to learning more about her, your relationship and yourself.

Now, translate this story into your own personal situations. When you experience a conflict or issue in your own life or in your mind, allow yourself to become a "Third Party Neutral." Step outside the situation, assume the role of "neutral" from both an internal position and from the other person's perception. Ask: "Why am I feeling this way? What's my side of the story? What's the other person's story? How's the other person feeling? What's the root cause of the conflict? What are our options? "

Champion Feedback

How can we possibly know ourselves in the absence of honest feedback from ourselves, as well as from others? One of the key skills and attitudes of a Third Party Neutral is that of receiving feedback from ourselves, in addition to being open to feedback from others. Feedback involves knowing our mind, body and soul.

Every action has a reaction or feedback. If an action is negative in some way and the feedback we give ourselves is honest, we can correct the negative action. In the same vein, if we deny the negative, and pretend a positive input, the problem will be amplified. We must confront and correct ourselves when warranted. We cannot do that unless we are as objective as possible about our own behavior.

Our own body is a prime feedback mechanism, constantly giving us signals about safety, truth, or anxiety. When a choice or action is right for us, we sense an increase in energy. When a situation is not safe or does not "ring true" for us, our body tells us so through pain, discomfort and sometimes even nausea. We simply must tune immediately to our first response in order to learn what options or choices are right for us. At that point, we either need to change our environment or change our response to it. We can develop the power to live our lives on a "want to, choose to" basis.

A confusing aspect of listening to your body is when the body's response is not about options, but about retreating into its comfort zone. It will require careful listening to distinguish that at times, for the body is a great advocate of comfort at almost any cost.

Assessment Instruments

When combined with other self-awareness methods, feedback through assessment instruments is often invaluable. There are plenty of excellent tools on the market to help you gain insight into who you are, your strengths and weaknesses, and how you relate to other people. These instruments are available at universities, psychological clinics, and personal development centers throughout the world. Certified practitioners employ these instruments and can help you with your own personal assessment interests.

Some of the best instruments include a 360-degree assessment instrument that facilitates feedback from family and colleagues, in addition to our own self-assessment. It's important to seek well-researched and tested products. For example, the Hermann Brain Dominance assessment tool is designed to gain insight into your brain dominance and thinking preference style. This instrument has been adequately researched.

Some assessment tools are self-administered and easy to use. CRG Resources of Abbotsford, British Columbia has designed, produced and distributes self-scoring, user-friendly instruments for assessing personality style, values, self-worth, health, and aptitude for mentoring, coaching, sales and marketing. I recommend you search the internet for further sources.

Clear Values

Self-awareness leads to being clear about your values. Are you able to "walk your talk" or live with integrity, be true to yourself? We each have different values, just as we each have a different make-up and varying primary needs. Your values strongly influence what you do and how you spend your time. Without first knowing what is most important to you, it is tough to make decisions or to set goals.

A value is something that has sufficient worth to you that you spend time trying to obtain it or keep it as part of your lifestyle. Being clear on your values assists you in choosing friends, business partners, making decisions and developing your short and long term goals resulting in greater balance and serenity in your life. Self-knowledge lays a rock-solid foundation for Self-Wealth.

When your mind, body and spirit are one, you are more grounded in your personality, more authentic, and you feel a greater identity and confidence in your worth. This builds trust in yourself and takes you a major step closer to wanting to take on new challenges. You can now move forward with coherence.

Application

Our values are the basis for all the decisions we make in life. Each of us places emphasis on certain values important to us, and our day-to-day activities reflect those values. For example, if contribution is a very important value in your life, you will probably engage in activities that reflect your desire to contribute to your community, some special group, or cause. A person who values spirituality above all else will probably spend as much time as possible reflecting on things, perhaps in meditation, and engaging in activities that reflect an emphasis on this important value.

With the demands of everyday life, what we truly value often assumes a back seat. In the following three-step exercise you will rank your top 7 values in order of importance and develop a plan to help you focus on what is most important to you. As you complete this exercise, also consider the results of exercises you have completed in earlier chapters. This should give you a broad perspective on where you are in your life now and the direction you want to go.

Step 1. Check off your values.

Study the list of possible values. If we've missed some values that are important to you, add them to the end of the list we provide. Select 7 values that are important to you by placing a check mark to the left of the 7 values.

Step 2. Rank your values.

Review those values you have selected. Rank these 7 values in order of importance, by numbering them from 1 to 7 to the right of each value, with 1 indicating your most important value.

Check 7 Top Values	Value	Rank 1-7
	Value Ranking	
___	Learning and Growing	___
___	Accomplishment	___
___	Intimacy	___
___	Spirituality	___
___	Security	___
___	Friendship	___
	Peace of mind, Serenity	___
___	Contribution	___
___	Creativity	
___	Organization	___
___	Challenge	___
___	Honesty	
___	Recognition	___
___	Fun/Pleasure	
___	Freedom/Independence	___
___	Community/Family	
___	Variety	___
___	_____	___

Step 3. Develop an Action Plan.

List the top 7 values you identified in step 2, and write down the action steps you will take to make each one a priority in your life.

	Action Plan	
Value	**Action I Will Take To Make it a Priority**	**When**
1.		
2.		
3.		
4.		
5.		
6.		
7.		

At a later date, reevaluate your life and determine if you are living up to your values. You may even discover that your values have changed over the course of time. As you change, your values may also change. Or at the very least, you may re-order your values, putting more emphasis on certain values over others.

Ultimately, the benefit of establishing your values is that it helps you focus more on how to get the most out of your life. This is an important part of the balance you can achieve in your life's journey towards Self-Wealth.

CHAPTER 8

Breaking Free:

Confront Self Limitations

"The worm that destroys you is the temptation to agree with your critics, to get their approval."

Thomas Harris

One of the most enduring myths of our time is that our emotions are an automatic response to situations in which we find ourselves, or a condition of our personality. Much of the advertising we are exposed to reinforces the notion that a product or service will make us feel better. This car, through its exceptional road handling, will make us feel in control. With this soft drink, we will get "the feeling." This medicine will provide emotional equilibrium.

Self-Wealth

At the very foundation of Self-Wealth is the acceptance that we control our thoughts, and that what we think produces our emotions. I don't mean that thoughts suppress our emotions. Our feelings are real and legitimate. However, no matter how harsh the circumstance *we are free to choose what we think.* We can *choose* whether our thoughts are self-defeating or self-enhancing. From that choice, our emotions will flow.

Dealing with Internal Beliefs

The first step in breaking free is to identify and confront the internal beliefs that sabotage you. If you examine your thoughts and feelings carefully, you may well find that you blame yourself for your own shortcomings. Well, here's the good news about that: acknowledging your short-comings is a great starting point for taking responsibility for your life!

Here's an example of how: you find a thought or belief within to the effect that "I can't make an effective presentation in front of a group. No matter how hard I try I just choke up. No wonder my career is stuck. It's my fault!"

Now, try this: "I accept responsibility for my own behavior. I admit freely that I have been frightened in the past when making a presentation to a group. When I think about it, I can understand my fright. I also can understand that my fright actually is what caused my presentation to fall short, despite my best preparation. From now on I am going to trust my ability. I know I am capable. I know my field. It's my responsibility to perform well and overcome those fears, and I *can* do it!"

Making this leap of faith in yourself will require practice. But its practice you can start *right now,* and work on daily.

Don't Punish Yourself

Here's a serious pitfall to look for as you begin to accept responsibility for your own outcomes. As you recognize how fully you have been involved in creating your own unhappiness, those negative feelings of blame and despair may lead to severe self-criticism. You must recognize that this negative cycle is what put you in the present situation, and seize control of that desire to torture yourself for past mistakes. Control the urge to punish yourself for not performing better before now.

Tell yourself in no uncertain terms that you did the best you could, given your understanding and experience, at the time. Treat yourself kindly, and reassure yourself that from now on, you're going to face reality squarely, and perform better. Keep telling yourself that each time self-blame begins to resurface. Acknowledge the shortcomings, and superimpose the knowledge that you are behaving differently from then on. Your subconscious is always listening, and every time you tell it that you are a more effective, more balanced person now—it moves to make you that way.

Re-framing

This re-framing of life experiences works both for past shortcomings and for day-to-day annoyances. As you move toward personal serenity, you will be freeing up enormous reserves of energy to apply toward achieving your personal goals. Here's a very common example:

153

You're waiting for a vehicle to leave a parking space. As it does, another driver barges in front of you to snatch the space. You think, "Who does he think he is? I've been waiting here. I would like to teach him a thing or two!" As you think this, your body responds, preparing for battle. Adrenaline is released into your blood stream; and your heart rate increases along with your blood pressure. Your emotions follow: you feel angry, cheated, frustrated and aggressive. You feel stressed.

But that's not you anymore. Imagine the same scene, using the new way of looking at things I'm discussing. You consciously realize that you have a choice as to how you view this rude behavior. So you frame your response this way: "That's really unfair, but it's not going to bother me. If I get angry and permit stress into my body, I allow another person's selfish behavior to shorten my life."

Or you could go a step further: "This person has just given me an opportunity to lengthen my life. I'll find a space farther away and get some extra exercise today. That guy's selfishness has certainly been of value." And you will walk the extra distance smiling to yourself.

Controlling Negative Thoughts

We control our feelings by working on the thoughts that precede them. We trap ourselves when we believe that events or people make us unhappy. It's simply not true. It is our *thoughts* about events or people that make us unhappy. Once we change our thoughts, different feelings will follow.

154

Negative thinking can strangle the meaning from our lives. Each of our lives is filled with countless wonderful opportunities. Yet almost all of us carry around a deep sense of resignation. The goals and opportunities we saw when we were young shrink until they fit with our disappointing experience. We begin to demand that our goals be workable, achievable, and if possible, guaranteed. When we can't see the likelihood of a favorable outcome, we become dispirited, with a sense of powerlessness about making a real difference in our own future, let alone that of others.

This is the much-cited life of quiet desperation. It is quiet because it is seldom discussed, especially if we possess some of the outer trappings of success. We expend a lot of energy maintaining the facade that our lives are "together." We worry about the way we look. Worry about what we own or possess. We worry whether we are doing enough. We tell ourselves that if we don't work harder we just won't make it. We feel guilty because somehow we just aren't good enough. We get so busy either "doing" or feeling bad because we aren't "doing", that we mistake motion for progress.

We miss the real opportunities that are right before our eyes. We live in this contradictory state of frenzied activity. We tread water, not going anywhere, but we are too scared to stop for fear of drowning. Our lives become meaningless, not because we planned them that way but because we haven't stopped to listen, to question, to pray, to love or simply (with profound effect) to be still.

Self-Wealth

Rising Above Your Circumstances

Throughout this book I have used the term Self-Wealth almost interchangeably to refer to internal balance, serenity, and material gain. The latter flows from the former. We break free from our self-limiting beliefs by confronting them, finding the thoughts that shaped them, and redesigning those thoughts into a form with which we are happier. It is a curious phenomenon that we must *feel* rich in order to become rich. We must learn to see with *unfettered* eyes the marvelous world of opportunity that lies around us every day. The seeds of your greatness are within your grasp right now. Either under your hand already—or known to you. All you have to do is perceive them correctly.

Perhaps you find yourself scoffing at this. Sure, you may say, easy for you to say—but I face little more than a barely adequate paycheck every month. Believe me, my friend, I have been there.

As long as you concentrate on the fact that last week's salary is practically gone before you get it, you are living in the *past*. You are instructing your subconscious precisely on how the future will be. Is that what you want? No? Then start re-framing those thoughts and the feelings will follow. Stop blaming your inability to earn enough for your needs, and accept responsibility for the fact that if you want something to change, the change starts with *you.*

Some Rise, Some Don't

Research over the last three decades has provided us with insight as to why some individuals rise above their circumstances and others don't. The beliefs that you hold about your capacity to perform, shape the course of your life. You will readily tackle situations and activities that you judge yourself capable of handling, and avoid those where you feel incapable. The key point is that if we don't believe we can perform in a new circumstance, we will avoid it. We will choose the status quo, to the point of actually sabotaging remarkable opportunities in our lives.

Beliefs about your performance stay locked in your thoughts long after the precipitating event is ancient history. Every time you think about or trouble yourself over a performance you consider unsatisfactory, it is as if you are experiencing that failure again. Rather than a sense of self-mastery and willingness to tackle a new challenge every time you see a new opportunity, your mind will dutifully supply you with the sorry track record you have lived in the past.

You Have the Power

It's up to you, and only you, to revisit those limiting beliefs and reframe them into a more positive light, which will free up energy to tackle the challenges you face today. Self-Wealth is a self-help plan—you root out those enduring negative beliefs and replace them with fresh vivid new images of the you that you now see yourself becoming.

Just the feeling you will gain from changing these old limiting beliefs will be amazingly liberating to you. You will walk with your head higher, look life in the face, and feel more personally valuable. People will notice, and begin to respond to this new you. You may notice to your surprise that that too-short paycheck no longer is the center of all your concerns. You have adjusted your thinking. You no longer are running from a fear of failure, but marching toward a sense of success. Your bank balance may not have changed a dime, but you will *feel* the difference.

You will be earning your own Self-Wealth through your own efforts. The feeling of empowerment is heady stuff, believe me. Should you then make the conscious choice to follow your personal sense of Self-Wealth with the actual material evidence of Self-Wealth, the opportunities will open before you.

I don't mean by this that you will buy a winning Lottery ticket. You will face many challenges on your path. But those challenges will be worthwhile and even fun. Self-Wealth is a journey, not a destination—and whoever said that getting there is half the fun, was probably underestimating the truth.

Who's In Control?

We all hear the people around us talking, acting as if they are controlled by the circumstances in which they find themselves. Here are two examples.

Charles is a practicing dentist. He has a financially successful practice but finds it more and more difficult to get up each morning. His feelings of anxiety have increased over the last year. He has considered changing careers to pursue his interests in business, but can't make the decision to change. He feels that his wife might not support him; that he should wait six years until his children have completed their education. His partners in the practice would feel he has dropped them in a critical phase of growth. In short, he feels trapped.

What would you do if you were Charles? Is your life situation similar? Apply the principles I have talked about to his case for a minute. Re-frame his situation. This isn't a trick question, and there will be no test. Just see if you can't find some options for Charles.

And how about Evelyn? She gives up her successful sales career to be with her young family. When her children enter school she applies to her previous company for re-employment. She's not hired. She's bitterly disappointed. She has relied on them to accept her back at any time, even making a place for her. She wonders whether she has lost her winning edge, and they sense her self-doubt. Two other firms that advertised positions at lower levels than her original one turn her down. She feels desperate; there just seems to be no way out.

But is that true? Even close to true? If you've read our book this far, you already have identified her self-limiting beliefs and negative thinking. Think about her situation for a minute. Learn to look at the options she might be missing.

These two examples actually could come into play for you later on your journey to Self-Wealth, because as you develop your own inner sense of peace and serenity, you will find abundant energy left over to help others begin their own journeys. That's called mentoring, and when you give of yourself as freely as you give of your financial resources, the returns you will receive will far outweigh anything you ever have imagined.

Making Choices

Life is about choice. We always have a choice, no matter what the predicament. It often feels like our situation is beyond our control or that we are out of control. The reality is we choose to stay in a job that is not satisfying. We choose to blame others for our circumstances. Our own thoughts are the prime cause of the feelings that take away the joy in our lives. This realization is not easy to accept, but by doing so we take back the control we have relinquished. If we are responsible for creating our own misery, then we can be responsible for converting it to joy.

The truth is that we are in total control of our lives.

Simply Being Myself

Why do we spend so much energy trying to be someone we are not? As soon as we take on a new job or are promoted we begin to think about how we will have to change ourselves to fit into the new role. We feel like we need to be someone different, that the real me is not good enough. It's like trying to squeeze into a jacket that was tailored for someone else. Why do we so often have the sense that to be effective we have to be someone who isn't us?

In striving to be successful, we often strive to be someone else. We build up walls around our hearts to hide the real us. This effort takes *so much* emotional energy to support. It is as if I need to apologize to the world about who I really am. The real me becomes smaller and smaller, until I'm not really sure who I am any more.

You Are Who You Want to Be

Think about this for a moment. You determine your worth. There is no need for explanation or justification to anyone else. Self-image is your ever-present shadow, your personal advisor and evaluator of your happiness and value. It's your inner picture of who you are and what you think of yourself. Your self-worth is critical to your breaking free.

Every belief that we hold about ourselves is sanctioned by us. No one can give us a belief about ourselves, unless we sanction it. It is not events that create our beliefs, it is the way we choose to interpret the events. The thoughts are recorded in our minds as "us." When we face new situations, we are not interpreting them from clean slates, but through filters consisting of our existing beliefs. We engage in internal conversations about ourselves in relation to this new information.

You and I are identical in one grand respect: I can only be free when I am authentic; always just me, never changing when I'm with different people who have different demands. The same holds true for you. I can only be at peace with myself when I accept myself as I am. I will not always meet your expectations. At times I will fail. You might even reject me. But I won't pretend to be someone I am not.

Think About the Real You

Stop and close this book after you read this paragraph and think about this for a moment. What goes through your mind when you think about the real you? Think back. When last did you have a sense of that real you? What was happening around you? What was triggered within you? How did you feel then? How do you feel right now? Have you permitted negative thoughts to erode the sense of who you are drastically? Learn to differentiate between those limiting beliefs—the thoughts—and you—the thinker of the thought.

The thought is not you. It is your property. It belongs to you. And only you can change it into something happier, more positive, more productive.

I Want to Change, but My Beliefs Prevent Me

This is the seeming paradox. We need to be ourselves. But what we conceive of as "ourselves" is almost loaded down with negative self-images. The psychologists call this "automatic thinking" and depressed people are notorious for it. The negative self-perception is so deeply ingrained that is mistaken for the true self.

Can we learn to separate our deep-seated negative beliefs about ourselves from our actual selves? The excellent news is that we can. If you take nothing else from this book, take this: you don't have to keep thinking poorly of yourself. You can change the way you think about yourself, and you can actually do it relatively fast. Believe me, this is the best use you can make of your time! Capture and identify those negative beliefs and re-frame them. Insist to yourself that those negative thoughts are not you. Your self will listen.

Listen to the things we tell ourselves.

" I was lucky to get the promotion."

"She said I was great because she knows that's what I want to hear."

Sound familiar? Many people tend to attribute value to anything but themselves. Your first step toward developing a strong sense of self-worth and finding serenity and balance in your life is to learn to recognize quickly everything you are telling yourself that could be construed as a put-down.

The second step is to immediately replace the negative with a constructive affirmation:

"I got the promotion because I deserved it."

"It's great that she appreciates me."

Folks, these flip-flops in your personal belief structure can occur as habitually as any other human endeavor and much faster than most. They merely take observation and practice.

We Control Messages

We are able to change because we have control over how we interpret messages we receive from others. We do not have to be victims of another person's negative influence. We have the power to choose what we receive and accept, and what we don't. As children this is not always the case, but as adults we get to choose what we believe. We are victims only if we make the personal choice to victimize ourselves. We have the ability to change our auto-pilot, *because we set it in the first place.*

Victor Frankl, the Viennese psychologist we discussed earlier, who survived the Nazi death camps, espoused this idea in *Man's Search for Meaning,* describing the horrid conditions there:

> "*We who lived in concentration camps can remember the men who walked through the huts comforting others, giving away their last piece of bread. They may have been few in number, but they offer significant proof that everything can be taken from a man but one thing: the last of*

163

the human freedoms—to choose one's attitude in any given set of circumstances, to choose one's own way."

The thoughts we hold about ourselves have taken years to ferment, so we can expect that it will take a bit of time for us to change them. But as we become aware of our internal self-talk, and actively change it when it is negative or counter-productive, the way we think slowly begins to change.

Your belief about yourself, and therefore your future, can be radically transformed and sustained. Persistence in re-framing your thoughts about yourself will provide a hundred-fold results.

Dealing with Dream Snatchers

One of the guarantees of personal change is that, once you begin to visibly improve, not everyone around you will be comfortable with your changes. Some people you thought you could count on for support may become your worst critics. Remember Barry Sefton? As he began to act on his life's dearest goal, and was successful, some of his closest friends couldn't handle it.

One of the saddest moments during his change was when he had to leave them behind. But he knew that if he didn't abandon all negative influences in his life, it would be like trying to move on with an anchor still tied firmly to the past.

Successful change has the potential to threaten others. Our change invariably means that others close to us will also feel the need to look at their own lives and possibly change. This can become very threatening. So, don't be surprised if those closest to you make every conceivable effort to force you back into your box in order to avoid having to exit or even acknowledge their own boxes.

You can anticipate that some people will attempt to snatch your dream the moment you begin to make it a reality. It was not a threat while it remained a dream. This kind of resistance often comes in the form of ridicule or personal criticism.

Our world is full of critics. Listen for a moment to the conversations we hear around us, how much of our social discourse is dedicated to criticism. Did you ever stop to think why someone criticizing the behavior of others was talking to you instead of the subject of the criticism? The real doers of the world have learned that destructive criticism is a waste of time. They won't sit still for it. They would rather be in the action. Successful individuals know that it's acceptable to make mistakes. While constructive criticism is invaluable to them, it takes no degree in psychology to discern the difference between constructive criticism and petty put-downs. The doers just move away from the latter—and go on doing. Try this technique yourself.

Dream snatchers prop themselves up at the expense of others. It's self-delusional and makes them a pain to be around. Avoid them if your truly aspire to Self-Wealth. Ask yourself two questions: Do I really need this right now, even if the person is important to me? Whose interest does he or she have at heart?

Sitting in Denial

Although it is often difficult to face our circumstances, it is downright painful to face ourselves. That's probably why we only tend to do so when triggered by some crisis. Death is a certainty for all of us. That's probably why the death of another affects us, and we pause in our lives, for a moment, to consider our own destinies.

Facing the reality of our own mortality is healthy. Facing the reality that tomorrow is not guaranteed can lead us from a place of complacency to doing something, taking action to change. Self-Wealth is about accepting the natural healthy tension that exists between our current reality and what we would like to be. Again, the point could not be more clearly illustrated than by Victor Frankl as he evaluated his experience in Auschwitz:

"One of the prisoners who on his arrival marched with a column of new inmates from the station to the camp, told me later that he had felt as though he were marching at his own funeral. His life had seemed to him absolutely without future. He regarded it as over and done, as if he had already died.

"A man who let himself decline because he could not see any future goal was occupied with retrospective thoughts. In a different connection, I have already spoken of the tendency that there was to look into the past, to help make the present with all its horrors less real. But in robbing the present of its reality there lay a certain danger. It became easy to overlook the opportunities to make something positive out of camp life, opportunities that really did exist. Regarding our 'provisional existence' as unreal was in itself an important factor in causing the prisoners to lose their hold on life; everything, in a way, became pointless. Such people forget that often it is just such an exceptionally difficult external

situation that gives man the opportunity to grow spiritually beyond himself. Instead of taking the camp's difficulties as a test of their inner strength, they did not take their life seriously and despised it as something of no consequence. They preferred to close their eyes and to live in the past. Life for such people became meaningless."

The concentration camps were an awful, ghastly, abnormal circumstance for any person to endure. It would seem logical to have denied current reality by focusing on the past or the future. Frankl found that both strategies failed those prisoners who employed them, because such thinking robbed them of emotional and spiritual resources to survive the horror of the present. To generate resilience to survive meant holding and keeping tension between their reality and future goals that they believed were critical to achieve in their lifetimes. For one prisoner it was the child who needed his father, for another the completion of a book.

To break free, we need to acknowledge and accept this tension. To live on the basis of memories is denial. To live in the dream world of a future is denial. To live each moment in the present as part of a purposeful future is to experience one of the cornerstone principles of Self-Wealth.

Lights, Camera—But No Action

So you've made a decision to change. But—similar to those New Year's resolutions—after a few weeks nothing much has happened. If you're like the rest of us, you do procrastinate. You put off doing things and then have to deal with all the negative feelings that result from not taking action. In such cases you end up with two problems.

First, the thing you committed to do is not yet done (and there's a pile of new things demanding attention now). Second, you feel bad or angry with yourself because one of the things you wanted to change about yourself was procrastination. You're in a vicious circle of your own making. We've all been there many times.

Procrastination is not just creative avoidance; it's living a lie. By saying we will do something in the future, we avoid facing the reality of doing something today. By intending to do something tomorrow or when we've finished this or that, we really say it's really not that important. We delude ourselves. By telling ourselves we will do something about something in the future, we distance ourselves from the reality that we are not doing something about it *now.*

Procrastination helps us delude ourselves into believing we are something other than we really are.

Sometimes we do finally get the something done, at the last minute and in far less time than we should or could have given it. But that is also a form of delusion because the limited time or energy finally given to the task often sanctions a "less than I'm worth result." We also put off action by waiting for some nebulous "right time," or until we feel right.

Since thoughts shape our feelings, and we don't like to think about painful or difficult actions, it is likely that if the action is painful or difficult, the time it feels right will never arrive. It is always best to judge ourselves on the basis of what we achieve, not what we intend. Others judge us not on our intentions but on our behavior.

As Emerson put it, "Your actions speak so loudly, I cannot hear what you say."

So if you want to change something, especially if it is personally critical, don't approach it as if you have the rest of your life, don't aim to do it in the long term. Face the fear that is holding you back from getting started. The best way to face that fear is to *start*.

Remember: The journey of a thousand miles begins with a single step.

Application

Here are some things to do *now*:

1. Take a serious look at your life. If you had six months to live (remember: you have absolutely no guarantees right now that you even have six days) what would you be doing?

2. Decide what you are avoiding in your life right now. What are the fears that are holding you back from living this moment more effectively? What old tapes do you need to stop playing in order to move forward?

3. Decide that your life is too precious to create extra stress for yourself by substituting the anxiety of a postponed future event for the value and wonder of the present moment. What do you need to do now? Right now?

CHAPTER 9

Trust and Let Go:

Capturing Synchronicity and Fortuitous Intersections in Your Journey

---

"Order your soul and trust in Providence."

Saint Augustine

Meaningful coincidences, and fortuitous intersections were around long before C.G. Jung published a book called *Synchronicity: An Acausal Connecting Principle* in 1952 and coined the term "synchronicity." Jung defined "synchronicity" as "a meaningful coincidence of two or more events, where something other than the probability of chance is involved."

Jung made synchronicity easier to understand by articulating three distinct characteristics. First, he proposed that the events are acausally connected. That is, the law of cause and effect cannot account for their occurrence. No one has planned these events. They are not intentional. Second, these situations are accompanied by a heart felt experience, either at the time of the event or later. Third, the events are often symbolic in nature.

Based on our own experience of synchronicity, my co-authors and I agree with those who believe that synchronicity is a *result* of being in a state of commitment and surrender. In other words, once we have committed to our purpose or goal bigger than ourselves and surrendered our control over the process of precisely how we're going to achieve it, synchronicity steps in and amazing assistance begins to emerge; this is, if we're watching for it.

When we commit to what we believe needs to happen, amazing things just start happening. We will explore the role of synchronicity, fortuitous intersections, and meaningful coincidences in the unfolding of life. They bring opportunities for insight, direction, intrigue, wonder and at times a sense of rapture to our lives. Always their value lies in the meaning that we actually take from them. They do indeed often redirect our life paths.

Whether such forces touch only lightly or significantly, sending our lives into new trajectories, they are an important dimension in maximizing our impact on the world. Some of us believe that God is in charge, and might refer to such events as divinely ordained incidents. Other readers may prefer a non-theological perspective, or explain them through psychology. Whatever our persuasion, there is no doubt that these situations have meaning and our lives are enriched through them.

In previous chapters we have discussed several ways and means of taking control of our lives. But you must understand that cognitive or behavioral skills alone do not determine our course in life. Career changes, divorces, accidents, illnesses, economic depressions, wars, technological revolutions and other social events do make our lives markedly different. And our lives can be strongly influenced by synchronicity and fortuitous intersections. Dr. Albert Bandura says, all things being equal, the ability to recognize and take advantage of fortuitous intersections—and to extricate oneself immediately from negative ones—is a significant factor in success.

Dr. Bandura has given this idea a good deal of consideration. In April 1981, his presidential address to the Western Psychological Association in Los Angeles was entitled, "The Psychology of Chance Encounters and Life Paths." His speech was subsequently published in the *American Psychologist* in July of 1982 and has since generated a great deal of interest. Dr. Bandura stated that fortuitous intersections touch all lives.

Let's look a little closer at this marvelous mechanism and how it works.

Acausal and Heart Felt

This story of my co-author Valerie Bates is a good place to start. At a very young age, she was stewing about whether to follow her peers and hitchhike across Europe in search of love, peace and highs, or follow the responsible path of teaching school. Feeling completely out of sync and utterly depressed,

172

she scoured the library, desperate for answers. Help came in the form of *Psycho Cybernetics*, by Dr. Maxwell Maltz.

"His life-changing book jumped out at me from the library shelf," Valerie says, " and I seized the opportunity to learn about positive thinking processes. I devoured the information."

Maltz, a plastic surgeon, developed a system for positive living based upon his patients' responses to re-constructive surgery. He concluded that in many cases the acquisition of a prettier face had little or no impact on one's level of happiness or self-esteem.

"Subsequently, I decided not to have that nose job after all," Valerie quips.

Studying *Psycho Cybernetics* led to a trajectory in her life that resulted in a series of synchronistic events

As a result of reading Maltz's book she decided to pursue a teaching career. It was well into the month of October, and the odds of finding a position at that time of year were slim to none. To her amazement, she found a newspaper advertisement for a teacher in a small Cree village called Pikwitonei, Manitoba.

"The adventure of a lifetime began on January 2, 1971," she says now, " and involved synchronicity at its finest"

Here's the rest of her story:

"The train was delayed due to a knifing in the village. I arrived in Pikwitonei late that evening and the school janitor guided me by flashlight to my home. Since there were no streetlights, I could discern little. In the light of day, the school janitor led me from my little teacherage over the pristine snow-ladened paths to visit students' homes.

"What left me utterly breathless and loudly expressing 'Ahaaaaa!' was the synchronicity of the situation. I noticed a

173

familiar scene—a tiny steeple church overlooking a river and surrounded by a white picket fence. I realized that this was precisely the village I had visited with a social worker friend two years earlier. We had landed on the frozen river and, descending from the plane, I declared that never had I seen such a beautiful, tranquil wonderland. I stated that I would give my left arm to live in this tranquil cozy wonderland. Little did I realize at the time that my request would be answered two years later."

This fortuitous intersection was to shape her life, offering an opportunity to develop skills and unlimited insights in a short period of time. Two of the most profound lessons centered on redefining loneliness and not succumbing to fear. She learned that two predecessors' experiences had proven fateful. She replaced a young teacher who had been raped. The teacher before that had hung himself in the cramped bedroom in which Valerie attempted sound sleep for what seemed like a lifetime before she achieved it.

Through that meaningful connection with Dr. Maltz's book, her life path was altered significantly. She built a strong sense of self-efficacy and wonder at the web of connectiveness in our world.

" I learned to survive," she reflects, "even if it meant staving off packs of wild dogs en route to school by swinging a broom wildly over my head. I coped with extreme loneliness by playing poker with trainmen, calling weekly Bingo, dancing the jig alone to out-of-tune fiddle music on Saturday nights.

All of this experience and wisdom came at the age of 20, triggered by two synchronistic events in her life.

Symbolic Signs Guide the Way

Fortuitous intersections act like signposts when we are "lost in the desert" and seeking direction or some indication of which road to take. They serve as symbolic confirmation and assure us that we're on track. Here's another story.

The Fourth of July long weekend was not a celebratory time for Marlene, Anne and David. They were beside themselves with worry over the impending bankruptcy of their once highly successful business. They had been living in denial for some time, and now realized that the writing was on the wall. Unless a miracle occurred to change a dire situation, the company would be out of business the following week. It was not only their problem, the livelihoods of countless families rested in resolving the situation.

They began to pray together and asked for help. They implored God grant them the wisdom to do what was right, and asked for a sign that help was on its way. They were sitting quietly in reflection when a loud hissing noise filled the room and a clock connected to the VCR flashed a red light indicating "7:30 A.M."

David said to his business partners, "I know this has meaning and connection with what we've prayed for, because that clock has never come on before. It was not set to do so. We have never even used that clock. There must be some significance to "7:30 A.M."

Anxious to give their problems one last go, they put the thought aside and began their next round of calls to potential investors and consultants. Richard, a highly recommended

175

consultant seemed quite promising. Arranging for a morning flight, Richard agreed to meet them in Los Angeles the following day. David asked Richard for details concerning his flight arrangements, anxious to hear him say 7:30 A.M. He learned that Richard's flight was to leave at 6:00 A.M. and concluded there was no connection after all. In the end, Richard's TWA flight was cancelled and he switched to an American Airline flight. The symbol was significant after all. His ticket and flight number read: AM 730.

Richard was as competent as they had hoped, and instrumental in salvaging the company through reorganization, refinancing, and acquiring sufficient investors. The partners became convinced that Richard was meant to be a business partner. He accepted their invitation, never realizing to this very day that synchronicity played such an important role.

Infinite Fortuitous Intersections

Some fortuitous encounters touch only lightly; others leave more lasting effects, and impact the lives of countless people in grave situations.

James Laue, founder of a well-known conflict resolution program with George Masson University in Fairfax, Virginia, played a major support role in the resolution of conflict within South Africa as a result of a fortuitous intersection in which he played no direct role.

My co-author, John, was involved in the mediation of conflict in South Africa. In vain, he searched South Africa to find expert help. Then he searched outside of Africa, but to no avail. He proceeded to make the best of a seemingly impossible situation; never anticipating that a solution would result from a fortuitous intersection with a total stranger.

It turned out that as John waited for lost luggage at Johannesburg International Airport, he overheard a heated argument between a disgruntled passenger and desk clerk. John casually commented to a stranger, whose luggage had been lost on an entirely different flight, that sometimes the conflicts we enter waste time and energy and help no one. A discussion about mediation ensued. The fellow traveler was an attorney involved in alternative dispute resolution. He told John about James Laue. John called Dr. Laue "out of the blue."

James Laue committed to do whatever it took to assist in South Africa. That included countless hours of long-distance phone consultation, and trips to South Africa at his own expense. Although numbers are hard to determine, numerous lives were saved as a result of the fortuitous intersection of two men with lost luggage from different flights.

Friends, Lovers and Business Partners

The skills and interests we develop determine the social circles in which we move and hence the kinds of social encounters we are likely to experience. People often intentionally seek certain types of experiences, but the persons who enter our lives are determined by a large element of chance. Interpersonal attraction seals chance encounters into lasting bonds. Ask people about the greatest fortuitous intersections in their lives, and often they will relate stories about love, friendship or business relationships that resulted from meaningful coincidences or fortuitous intersections.

Consider Tannis Helliwell, author of *Take Your Soul to Work*. Her life is filled with such intersections, and she is always attuned to their occurrence and prepared to discern their meaning. In addition to working as a corporate consultant for organizations like IBM and the Banff School of Management, Tannis leads tours to sacred sites throughout the world. Each year when she has completed a tour, she meditates to determine where the next tour should be conducted. For years she wanted to go to Japan. The challenge was to find an experienced guide who was spiritual, an excellent translator, and available in May. It seemed a daunting task, but a meaningful coincidence stepped in to solve the dilemma.

One blustery, rainy day, Tannis and a friend decided to escape the city of Vancouver, B.C., and experience the beauty of Mount Baker in Washington State. As they drove up the mountain, the rain grew heavy. Worried about driving over the steep edge of the road, they parked the car and walked the winding narrow route up the mountain. As they walked, they prayed that they would find the right guide to lead them on their journey to sacred sites in Japan. Two men were walking behind them. One was wearing a headscarf bearing Japanese characters.

"Is that Japanese writing on your scarf?" Tannis asked.

"Yes, I just returned from Japan three weeks ago," he answered.

"What were you doing there?" Tannis inquired further.

"I've led tours there and translated Japanese for the past five years, " he replied.

"I organize and lead tours to sacred sites," Tannis said. "Our next expedition is to Japan during the month of May. Are you available and interested in leading sacred tours?"

His answer was a resounding yes. Not only was the timing right, he had a personal goal to lead spiritual tours, and this would be his opportunity to realize a dream.

The guide hesitated for a moment and added, "there's just one logistical problem. I'm not from here. I'm from Vancouver."

Tannis responded, "So am I!"

Was this encounter "an accident"?

What do you think?

Surrendering the Means – Letting Go

We must be determined in our goals, yet willing to alter our course when our plans are consistently stymied, or a chance encounter and coincidence shows us something other than what we had expected.

Sometimes we don't recognize situations as fortuitous encounters that will change the course of our lives until later in life, when the whole story has unfolded and the road has lead to development of our character. Such is the case with Eileen Hendry, formerly a colleague of Valerie Bates' with the Center for Executive and Management Development in British Columbia. What appeared as utter devastation ultimately became, for Eileen, a fortuitous intersection.

For seven years Eileen worked her way through an undergraduate degree in Psychology at McGill University in

179

Montreal, paying her way by managing the International Clinic for McGill's Allan Memorial Institute of Psychology, a training ground for multi-national interning psychiatrists. While there, she became a friend and protégé of several women psychologists/social workers.

She decided to follow in their footsteps with a graduate degree in social work and juggled three jobs in order to earn enough money to study full time. She vowed to escape the controversy between the French and English in Quebec, and moved to Vancouver to study at the University of British Columbia. Upon settling there, she was devastated when her plans were stymied. She had not been accepted into the graduate psychology program. She literally felt that her life had fallen apart.

Eventually, a guidance counselor guided her into studying at the Faculty of Education in the Psychology Department. This compounded fortuity of the Quebec situation forcing her move, the rejected application, and the guidance counselor's spontaneous intervention at a critical point, set a career path for Eileen that ultimately led to a life filled with the variety and challenge of helping others develop their potential. Had just one of those factors not been present, her life career would have taken an entirely different course. However, because of this synchronicity, Eileen broke barriers for women in the workplace and business long before it was popular to do so. She influenced countless women to grow professionally, express opinions and demonstrate confidence in their expertise.

At that time, men were mentored, yet women were not. Eileen established a mentoring program for women along with a support system called the Women's Network that continues to flourish today. Since then, Eileen has continued to influence the lives of countless women and men through advanced leadership development programs and her private counseling practice. A fortuitous intersection sending Eileen's life path into a trajectory she had not planned, and one that she had originally considered a disastrous predicament, triggered all of this.

Understanding the role of fortuitous intersections allows us to more readily accept situations in which our own desires fail to be realized because something beyond us has intervened.

Recognizing Fortuitous Intersections

Fortuitous intersections or synchronistic events are not something for which we search. They are a *result* of a certain mindset or mental model we have of the world as one of interconnectivity. They are much like creating a work of art such as a great painting or sculpture. In order to create a masterpiece, we must let go of preconceived ideas about that masterpiece and create as the motivation and inspiration appear. We must "go with the flow."

By knowing ourselves, committing to our bigger goal in life, surrendering to the process and then being alert to opportunities, we can allow life to unfold as it was designed in accordance with the laws of natural order.

Application

1. Think back to events in your life that you would consider fortuitous intersections or synchronistic events. What impact have they had on your path?

2. Ask others about their experiences with intersections and learn as a result of your discussions.

3. Be ever alert for the emergence of fortuitous intersections in order to benefit from them.

CHAPTER 10

Keep it Simple, Stupendous!:
It Really is Simpler Than You Might Think!

"Simplicity is the ultimate sophistication."

Leonardo de Vinci

Dr. Emily Cady was one of the few women who persevered to become a medical doctor early in the twentieth century, when many obstacles were placed in that career path for women. Later she penned several philosophical works. In one, *Lessons In Truth*, we found a sentence that became our personal battle cry in creating a workable system for teaching Self-Wealth.

"Simplicity is evidence of the most advanced teachings," Dr. Cady wrote.

In this book, we have made every effort to spell out our principles simply. Dr.Cady was right. If our ideas cannot be explained clearly and concisely, we obscure them from those without advanced vocabularies.

Our purpose here is not to re-invent the wheel. We have integrated newer laboratory research findings with many of the concepts identified and described in academic research over the past few decades. Our purpose is to strip universally applicable ideas of their mask of academic rhetoric and speak plainly.

We have no quarrel with the convoluted "academic script" in which the highly educated write; it is almost a separate language, and they write mostly for other academics. Many PhDs have a horror of writing in simple English. They even have a term for it: "popular" style writing. Unfortunately, academic writing often conceals very good ideas from the rest of us.

Andrew Carnegie's Largesse & Napoleon Hill:

Many have pondered the question of what makes for true success in this life. One of the most famous of those was Andrew Carnegie, the poor Scots immigrant who became a mega-millionaire and gave a lot of it away; scores of communities across America received their first public library through Carnegie's largesse.

Carnegie commissioned a newspaper reporter with the grand name of Napoleon Hill to interview the wildly successful people of his generation and find a common denominator for their achievements. Hill wrote a book called *Think and Grow Rich*, one of the first "popular" volumes to address methods of using correct thought processes to impact success levels. A line from Hill's book, "You become what you think about," fired the imagination of a young broadcast journalist named Bill Nightingale, who applied that principle to his own career and built a hugely successful business selling motivational products to generations of North Americans.

Our thinking on achieving success, is laid out for you in this book, as simply as possible. These are the principles and tools refined from our collective experience and all the books and articles and research we waded through in preparation for putting together the book you hold in your hands. We found nothing so complex we had to use fancy words to describe it.

We sought to keep it simple. And that's our parting message to you: *Keep it Simple, Stupendous.*

Yes, this is a takeoff on the well-known: Keep it simple, Stupid. But "stupid" is negativism personified. Taking concepts that are otherwise complex, and simplifying the approach to understand them, is a rather sophisticated task. Therefore, simplicity in this context, as Dr. Cady exhorted, is actually quite advanced.

Some of you may be wondering, "Where do I begin with Self-Wealth?" Follow our complete system comprised of the principles discussed in this book. Ignore any one of these and you may not achieve Self-Wealth. The principles are synergistic or work together to create prosperity, balance and serenity in your life. We call this, "A Systems Approach to Self-Wealth" in order to emphasize the need to apply all nine principles in your quest.

So let's review the material covered with the aim to provide you a simple overview to keep in mind. In fact, it may prove beneficial for you to refer back to this chapter time and again, to refresh your memory. Study the following circle diagram which summarizes the nine principles. The three outcomes of Self-Wealth: prosperity, balance and serenity are identified in the outer ring of the circle.

185

Systems Approach

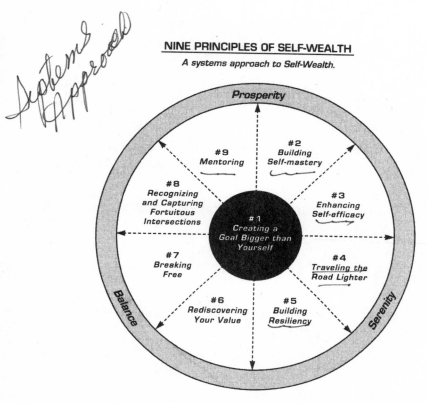

NINE PRINCIPLES OF SELF-WEALTH
A systems approach to Self-Wealth.

Unleashing your full potential through awareness, attitude and action.

Principle #1 Creating a Goal Bigger Than Yourself

First of all, we have defined Self-Wealth. Self-Wealth begins with your internal sense of worth. In order to put your own life on the high road to Self-Wealth, find a cause larger than yourself, something to which you can dedicate all your energies. The worthiness of the endeavor will reflect your own self-worth, and you will attract whatever you want and need into your life to fulfill your purpose.

Principle #2 Building Self-mastery

Next we discussed self-mastery, and how mastering your fears and phobias in any area can have a very positive "spill-over" effect into other areas of your life. If you have not had self-mastery experiences, or have not regarded them as such, challenging opportunities lie all around you for obtaining these experiences and developing a solid core of self-mastery.   Again, nothing very complicated in this: pick an activity, do it, feel the success, enjoy the strengthened sense of accomplishment.

Remember our stories about Barry Sefton and Nelson Mandela? Persistence!

Volumes have been written about persistence; nothing will take its place. You focus on your goal and keep going toward it, and don't let setbacks or naysayers or your own internal yearning for a (miserable but safe) comfort zone deter you. Having a goal larger than yourself—and a sense of self-mastery—will increase your ability to be tenacious and keep going. It really is as simple as that.

Principle #3 Enhancing Self-efficacy

Ah, those comfort zones. The term is derived from a thermostat, which kicks in to maintain a preset temperature whenever the ambient temperature moves too far one way or the other. Maybe it should be renamed *the quiet-desperation zone*. One of America's earliest philosophers, Henry David Thoreau, noticed that most people lead lives of "quiet desperation." We have talked about how our own thoughts set this mental temperature. We can very simply

187

begin to change that setting by *listening* to these automatic thoughts which have lodged in our minds at random over our lives, and *reshape* them through affirmations into thoughts we *want* to have.

Self-mastery, mental and physical health, vicarious experiences and eternal validation all build self-efficacy. Confidence in your own power to produce results is what self-efficacy is all about.

Principle #4 Travelling the Road Lighter

There's nothing complicated about how we all allow others to dictate our feelings through their attitudes about us. Nor is it difficult to understand how chance encounters influence our lives. The fact that we use other peoples' feelings about us to dictate our successes in life doesn't seem difficult to understand. We used the metaphor of a backpack full of stuff, getting heavier as we make our way through life. To move faster and lighter on the way to Self-Wealth, it is necessary to examine the contents of that backpack, no matter where they came from, and jettison all that unnecessary weight.

As you work through the applications and sample exercises in this book, you will find that you can haul that stuff out and leave it behind. The lighter your load, the faster you move. Simple as that.

It's never too late to start. It doesn't matter how heavy your backpack is, or how solidly you are ensconced in your "comfort" zone. *You* get to decide. You can start right now, right this minute, to "own" your thoughts. They're yours. And since you own them, you can discard any that do not serve you, and replace them with thoughts that do. We've given you easy-to-understand tools for making dramatic progress in your endeavors. Whenever you feel yourself slipping, go back to the appropriate chapter and refresh your memory of the basics. And start over.

Principle #5 Building Resiliency

What do you trade for a comfort zone in order to build resiliency? How about a transition zone?

Danaan Parry was Valerie's favorite mentor, although they never met. Parry taught her through his writings and his example that you can't mentor yourself or others until you <u>"turn the fear of transformation into the transformation</u> of fear." We're saddened that Danaan died just days before receiving his international recognition for achievements in peace building. Please read now Danaan's parable of the trapeze:

> *"Sometimes I feel that my life is a series of trapeze swings. I'm either hanging on to a trapeze bar swinging along or, for a few moments in my life, I'm hurtling across space in between trapeze bars.*
>
> *"Most of the time, I spend my life hanging on for dear life to my trapeze-bar-of-the-moment. It carries me along, at a certain steady rate of swing and I have the feeling that I'm in control of my life. I know most the right questions and even some of the answers.*
>
> *"But, every once in a while as I'm merrily (or even not-so-merrily) swinging along, I look out ahead of me into the distance and what do I see? I see another trapeze bar swinging toward me. It's empty and I know—in that place in me that knows—that this new trapeze bar has my name*

189

on it. It is my next step, my growth, and my aliveness coming to get me. In my heart-of-hearts, I know that, for me to grow, I must release my grip on this present, well-known bar and move to the new one.

"Each time it happens to me I hope (no, I pray) that I won't have to let go of my old bar completely before I grab the new one. But in my knowing place, I know that I must totally release my grasp on my old bar and, for some moment in time, I must hurtle across space before I can grab onto the new bar.

"Each time, I am filled with terror. It doesn't matter that in all my previous hurtles across the void of unknowing, I have always made it. I am, each time, afraid that I will miss and that I will be crushed on unseen rocks in the bottomless chasm between bars. I do it anyway. Perhaps this is the essence of what the mystics call faith experience. No guarantees, no net, no insurance policy, but you do it anyway because somehow to keep hanging on to that old bar is no longer on the List of Alternatives. So, for an eternity that can last a microsecond or a thousand lifetimes, I soar across the dark void of the 'past is gone, the future isn't here yet.' It's called 'transition.'

"I have come to believe that this transition is the only place that real change occurs. I mean REAL change, not the pseudo-change that only lasts until the next time my old buttons get punched. I have noticed that, in our culture, this transition zone is looked upon as a 'nothing,' a place between places. Sure the old trapeze bar was real and that new one coming towards me, I hope that's real too. But the void in between? Is that just a scary, confusing, disorienting

190

nowhere that must be gotten through as fast and as unconsciously as possible? NO! What a wasted opportunity that would be.

"I have a sneaking suspicion that the transition zone is the only real thing and the bars are illusions we dream up to avoid the void where the real change, the real growth occurs for us. Whether or not my hunch is true, it remains that the transition zones in our lives are incredibly rich places. They should be honored, even savored. Yes, with all the pain and fear and feelings of being out of control that can (but not necessarily) accompany transitions, they are still the most alive, growth-filled, passionate, expansive moments in our lives." (from *Warriors From The Heart*, used with permission from Earthstewards Network: Baimbridge Island, Washignton 98110)

In order to persevere, you must be resilient. No failure or reverse is permanent if you won't let it be. You just consider it good training and move on toward your goal again. It's part of building success. Use the Solicited Critique Method to confront failure. Recognize that failure cannot occur until one quits. It doesn't matter if your house is lost in a sheriff's sale, or your car is repossessed. It really doesn't. Not if you can maintain your resiliency, your own internal sense of self-worth, keep your eye on your larger goal and use the TIC System. There will be other houses, other cars—if those are what you need on the path to your goal.

Self-Wealth

Principle #6 Rediscovering Your Value

That sense of self-worth is all-important. You've read a good deal about how to improve yours in these pages. Remember: it's a lifetime journey, something you need to focus on each and every day. It's never a done deal. Every day offers challenges that can reinforce or undermine your sense of yourself—depending upon how you perceive those challenges. Use the notion of being a Third Party Neutral to find a balance between action and reflection.

You really do become what you think about. What are you in the process of becoming? What will you become tomorrow? Part of discovering your own value is being clear on your values. Being true to yourself means you "walk your talk". Your values strongly influence what you do and how you spend your time. When we act on what we believe, we build trust in ourselves. Trust leads to confidence.

Principle # 7 Breaking Free

If, as you have been reading this, you have felt a sense of dissatisfaction with who you are and where you are right now, that's actually positive. That's what we call cognitive dissonance. Those are two fancy words, but the meaning is simple. Your present external reality doesn't match your internal desire for yourself. Recognizing that simple fact is important to change. Don't fear the tension created by that realization; such tension is a wellspring of energy to change. Examine the self-defeating beliefs you have internalized; sort them out; replace them with new positive statements of intent, full of passion and belief.

It's all about choice. You can read these words—or any others about unleashing your full potential—and sigh and close the book and lie down and wait until that tension winds back down to the level of quiet desperation. Maybe watch some TV until your mind is numb again. Or you can choose, right now, today, to make that first small step. It won't all come overnight or in a year or a lifetime. It's a *life* decision we're talking about. We always have a choice, no matter what the predicament. We are in total control of our lives. Facing the reality of our own mortality is healthy and often moves us from complacency to acting on what's most important in our lives. Do you want to take responsibility for your life, now, today, and start remolding it nearer to your heart's desire? *What is* your heart's desire? Have you given up even thinking about things like that? We haven't. That's our choice. What's yours?

The Comfort Zones of Those You Love

If you do decide to make major life-changing decisions, be prepared for negative reactions from those around you, who are accustomed to seeing you as part of a stable environment. You have been a predictable part of their own comfort zones. Anger, disbelief and hostility are some of the powerful emotions that can be aroused in frightened family members.

What if you've got a sixteen-year-old who expects you to fund an expensive four years of college? A spouse who's accustomed to a new BMW every so often and summer trips to Hawaii? And now you want to change your life in ways that may impact theirs?

If a career change is what you have in mind, you might assemble the family and say something like this:

"I'm miserable in my work. In addition to finding very little time for each of you, I spend 70-hour weeks in sheer boredom. I'm getting

193

old too soon. I dread the very thought of getting out of bed in the morning. My life isn't working, gang, and I want you to know that I both expect and need your complete emotional support, because I am going to make some changes that might involve changing jobs or even careers."

Even if the family is initially supportive, "practical" considerations will kick in. Which is to say their personal thermostats will be going crazy. They may have fears like the fear of loss of security. Here are some more suggested comments:

"You know it may seem risky for me to make a change. But there really is no such thing as risk. Here we are, hurtling through space at 63,000 miles per hour on a tiny speck of dust called Earth toward God-only-knows-what peripheral reaches of a constantly expanding universe—and all my friends are worried about their pensions! The best thinkers who ever lived tell us that the only lasting and abundant wealth is achieved by those engaged in work they love.

"Well, I don't love the work I'm doing. In fact, I hate it.

"Now, I don't plan on burning any bridges today and I'm not quitting tomorrow. But I am going to think hard about how to create the money we need in a different way—a way I do love. And I intend to act on what I decide. I'm good at what I do, even though I hate it, and the worst thing that can happen is that I don't succeed at my new endeavor and I return to what I'm doing now to support our family. But I really believe I will be happier and eventually far exceed my income by moving to a field I love. So, can I count on your support?"

You may not get their support immediately. You may encounter fear-motivated hostility. But you have laid it out in simple language. The key to change, involving other people who depend on you, is to

194

involve them in the process. As they see the improvements in you, your happiness will be reflected in them if they truly love you.

There is a grim side to this scenario that we would be remiss in not touching on. If your sincere requests for assistance in your new path are ignored or disrespected, you will face some very hard choices. Remember the French painter, Gauguin, who had to flee a respectable life in Paris for the South Seas before he could create his masterpieces?

That is the extreme other end of the scale. But we state this flatly: your life and ours are too short to spend in pursuits that make us miserable because those who depend on us prefer their comfort to our happiness, at any expense.

Again, it is your choice. You can continue to negotiate and find some compromise, you can surrender and move back into your assigned role, or you can walk away—at least temporarily—until you have followed your dream.

The Power of Dreams

"Dreams have power." Consider my friend who grew up loving to fish. Throughout high school and college, everyone made fun of him for opting to fish each weekend, often to the exclusion of dating. By age 20 he had developed a new kind of bass fishing lure, which his father agreed to stock in his 30-liquor-store chain.

The lures sold like hot cakes and Johnny reinvested his profits in other fishing items. By age 22 Johnny was fishing 40 hours a week to test his new inventions. Today, 30 years later, he owns the largest bass-boat manufacturing facility in the world and the largest four-block square sporting goods empire anywhere in North America. Johnny Morris became a self-made millionaire by parlaying his favorite hobby into a career. If he can accomplish that as a fisher,

195

what can you do with the activity you love most? It's simple, once you catch on.

Wren Helwig grew up in the Midwest. Wrennie, as I call him, had no particular artistic bent, but when a local glass blower announced that he needed an assistant, Wrennie applied. Within two summers he was making elaborate masterpieces. By the third summer, he decided to become a full-time glass blower, hardly a mainstream profession.

Many in his family bristled at the notion that this brilliant young man, destined for veterinarian school, was throwing his life away to live in the backwoods of Missouri and blow glass.

Today, 30 years later, Wren's glass art is sold in fine New York and London galleries. He lives in a palatial home overlooking beautiful Tablerock Lake, where he works six months a year and plays with his family the other six. Wrennie often earns in excess of half a million dollars a year, but what's critical to him is the free time he enjoys with his family. Wrennie Helwig has a balanced, Self-Wealth lifestyle. There is no doubt he believes this is due to his decision to pursue what he loves, and let somebody else doctor the horses. Furthermore, both Johnny and Wrennie put emphasis on those people in their lives who encouraged and supported them, and those who were not counterproductive to their goals early on.

The Age Factor

Ah, you say, but these examples were people who began early and took decades to perfect careers they loved. That's true, but it's much easier at age 30, 40, 50 or beyond to succeed at a new career! Why? Because your maturity has given you all the tools. I switched from the ministry to a business I loved, and created a $10 million income over the next decade. I was 36, fed up with the ministry, and had always wanted to be a sales trainer and author. To start as a young man and reach this goal would have taken thirty years. Yet within six months of becoming a network marketer, I was earning $30,000 a month. Six months after deciding to become an author, I hired an accomplished author to mentor me. Within a year I had a best-seller on my hands.

If you complicate the process of Self-Wealth, you'll probably never take the steps necessary to launch your joy-filled career—no matter how old you are. Forget all the excuses that have kept you tied to your present life and get started.

Principle #8 Recognizing and Capturing Synchroncity and Fortuitous Intersections

When you move determinedly on a course of your own choosing, do not be surprised if the universe seemingly moves to accommodate you. It's one of those marvelous mysteries of the universe that this is so. We talked at length about fortuitous intersections and synchronicity; these things exist as surely as does gravity. If you jump, gravity brings you back to earth. If you move out smartly toward worthy goals larger than yourself, fortuitous intersections will open the path for you. Recognize opportunities and act on them. Let go of the process and "go with the flow."

Principle #9 Mentoring

Finding a suitable mentor is crucial in paving the road to Self-Wealth. A mentor will help you avoid the long route to developing your unlimited potential. Just imagine the benefits of having a person who has been very successful in your field of endeavor act as a guide, advocate and teacher to you.

Here's what to look for in a mentor, in addition to their having expertise in your field. These are the same qualities you should possess someday when you become a mentor:

Congruent and credible. Find a mentor who is a genuine sort of person who keeps his or her commitments. She will need to step down from her pedestal if she is going to mentor you effectively. Sometimes her role will involve confrontation and the straightforward expression of her own feelings — both negative and positive. An effective mentor will live what she preaches, in other words, she is credible.

Caring and prizing. Compassion and caring are at the heart of mentoring. Make sure your mentor has a nurturing attitude, and understands that new thoughts and productive processes emerge and take root more readily in an accepting climate.

Empathetic. Your mentor will help you develop growth-promoting attitudes towards yourself. He will achieve this by listening empathetically, and responding in a nonjudgmental way. A good mentor will always seek to guide and to encourage you.

- **Affirming.** Painting positive scenarios or pictures of what can be based on her own wisdom culled from experience is a habit your mentor must exercise. He will plant seeds in your mind about who you are and what you are capable of being. He will validate and affirm you in such a way that that you begin to "own" the affirmations.

- **Celebratory.** Too often we move through our successes without cementing the images into our subconscious so that they build efficacy. A great mentor will ensure that you take time to celebrate and reflect upon your successes, and share and affirm them until you accept them as your own and grow from them.

Six Simple Steps in Getting Started

Here are six specific steps to make your transition both simple and stupendous:

Step One: Focus on those things you most enjoy doing as an avocation, or invent some. Spend at least one month thinking things through. No one would set sail for France without a series of maps, charts and specific plans. But few people, it seems, actually give serious

199

thought to those activities that bring joy and serenity to their lives.

People have no sense of direction, because they dismiss the possibility that they could actually earn an effective living doing what they enjoy. And that they could contribute in some meaningful way to others, which is the only real source of personal satisfaction. So step one is to figure out what you <u>do</u> enjoy and in what way you want to make a difference in the world.

Step Two: Begin a research phase. It can be a great deal of fun to seek out others who have made a successful career in a field that interests you. Simply reading about others who have dared to pursue what you love as their primary profession will begin to solidify the vision and possibilities in your own mind. Go find books and articles that describe the field you love. Notice how countless folks have built successful careers around the very things you've never considered practical.

Step Three: During your visionary and research stages, begin searching for a mentor. This is a tremendously important step. So, don't skip it. A mentor will help you develop both from a personal and professional perspective. A mentor will have earned respect and is a recognized authority in your preferred field. Keep in mind that most people who are unusually successful in their given profession are probably much sought after and are very busy people. But keep on looking. Stay with it.

Step Four: Contact your mentor by telephone, letter, e-mail or fax and explain sincerely how much you would appreciate help. Successful people often are the very best of people, with compassionate hearts and a willingness to share their knowledge with those who sincerely and openly seek their wisdom. And you never know, but they could very well open some doors of opportunity for you as well.

Here's a sample letter you might use as is, or create your own letter using this example as a guide:

Dear ...

Although my friends and family question my sanity for leaving a high paying profession, I'm just not happy. I would rather be doing what you do. In order to get started, I need a mentor. I need a person of your stature to coach me along the way so I can avoid mistakes. As you can well imagine, I have tremendous financial obligations and therefore cannot afford to make numerous mistakes. I don't have a lot of money to pay for your personal mentoring, but I do have commitment and plenty of potential.

I realize how busy you must be. I promise not to abuse your time. I am so committed to getting help that I am willing to travel to your city and buy you lunch for just an hour of your precious time in order to explore possibilities. On the other hand, perhaps an hour on the telephone would be easier for us to break the ice and get to know one another in exploring a potential relationship.

I need your help. It is my fondest dream that one day a young person who respects me as much as I respect you will ask for my mentoring. When that happy day comes, I promise you I will help them exactly as I am asking to be helped now.

I am open to any method that suits your convenience, if you should agree to mentor me. If so, I will make myself available at any time of the day or night.

I am eagerly anticipating your response.

Sincerely,

Provide your phone number at the close of the letter, an e-mail address or a FAX number. You can also indicate that you plan to make a future phone call as a follow up to the letter.

If your first choice does not respond, or turns you down, find another. Practicing resilience and perseverance is important even at this stage of your experience.

Take heart, there *is* a successful person in your chosen field out there, right now, who feels the need to pass along her hard-earned wisdom. Believe in synchronicity, and keep looking!

Step Five: Begin to systematically plan your future. Make use of the personal coaching you receive from your mentor.

Step Six: Keep your family advised throughout as you move through the steps. Remember to keep your efforts simple. Once you've followed steps one through six you are ideally positioned to begin your effort, perhaps part-time at first, in any field of your liking.

It will be a challenge, given the internal boundaries you may have drawn in the past, as well as the external pressure from loved ones who feel that their security blanket is slipping away. But for thousands, including us, this march towards Self-Wealth has proven quite manageable, and even fun.

The Self-Wealth journey is ongoing and never complete. New opportunities and discoveries constantly emerge. One key opportunity will be your chance to mentor others. Take up this challenge and discover the joy of giving of yourself to others.

To restate the theme of this whole chapter: keep it simple and you'll be stupendous!

Application

1. Select three to five endeavors that would lead to an enjoyable career. Also create a list of several worthwhile contributions you can make to other people.

2. Write them down in their order of priority. Pull the sheet out three times a day and form a mental image of your actual participation in each field. We have written such lists on index cards or stickies and posted them in various places throughout our homes.

3. Take action today. Conduct research, find a mentor, and do something in the direction you want to be.

Afterword

You stand at the beginning of what will undoubtedly become one of the most significant periods in the history of humanity. We are poised at the edge of this New Millennium with tremendous personal and global possibilities. Each of us have the opportunity to dramatically re-shape our own lives and the lives of others unlike ever before. You are entirely capable of experiencing prosperity, serenity, and a marvelous sense of personal fulfillment in your life. And this can enable you to help others experience these same desirable qualities of life. You can make changes in ways that our grandparents could never even imagine. The technologies for personal change as we have outlined in this book are just a part of the process. Ultimately, however, the responsibility to take action, and make a change in your own life, begins with you.

The fact is, there have always been two types of people: those who think they can, and those who think they can't; and they're both right. Think about it. Which type of person are you? This is an important question, because it can have a dramatic impact not only on your life, but very likely on the lives of many other people. Because one person, with the right attitude and willingness to make positive things happen, can impact the lives of many, who in turn can impact even more lives.

When Nelson Mandela went straight from a tiny prison cell to the office of the President of his great nation, there was an almost collective global sigh of awe as everyone marveled at the perseverance of one man. No doubt countless others throughout the world drew strength and encouragement from what this man achieved.

Our Mission

My co-authors and I hope that in some way, this small book, and our desire to teach its contents to people everywhere, will change the lives of countless people everywhere. It is our heartfelt commitment to try to help others escape the shackles of the comfort zones of their own making. You are not the victim of your circumstances, unless you *choose* to be. There really is nothing that stands in the way of anyone who is resolved to change herself and her circumstances. We believe that whoever you are, whatever your color, age, sex, citizenship, or experience, you can dramatically enhance your own life and the lives of others. We believe that through self-mastery experiences, synchronicity, self-efficacy techniques, the correction of self-limiting beliefs, and other Self-Wealth principles, you can achieve literally every dream and goal you can conceive.

We also believe, during the course of your journey, you will discover that it is the experience itself that is most rewarding. To experience Self-Wealth is not just a goal, it is a journey. That is *true* Self-Wealth. In other words, Self-Wealth is as much a state of mind as it is a destination and a set of circumstances.

Whatever you do, please do not spend your life trying to live up to the expectations of other people—otherwise known as impression management. More than likely, the critics and the naysayers are not the creators and the doers. Dare to shun the criticism as you strive forward, do not be content to sit on the sideline of life as a spectator. Dare to risk embarrassment and setbacks. That's just part of the process. Dare to cling to your values and morals, in spite of what the rest of the world believes.

You are everything you've always thought was great about others and much more, so go out and demonstrate it. The time is now, and the whole world is waiting.

Invitation for Stories

We work with many people either in seminars, at speaking engagements, during phone consultations, conferences, and so on. One of the most exciting and rewarding aspects of our work comes in the interaction we have with people. Most exciting of all is when we learn from people that the Self-Wealth principles outlined in this book have changed their lives. That is what we are all about, and that what Self-Wealth is all about. It is about changing lives.

I have always found that the most inspiring things in life are often the stories people share about their unique experiences. This is what reaching out to others involves. We can learn so much from each other. It is particularly inspiring to hear about people overcoming obstacles in their lives. When it comes to making dramatic changes in your life, such as changing a career and pursuing dreams, sometimes the only way some people gather the courage to get started and the inspiration to keep going are the stories and encouragement they receive from others of like mind.

If you have a story you would like to share with us, please write. We read everything and plan to put new stories in our newsletter, and in the next edition of this book. To contact us, the best thing to do is to write, care of my publisher at the following address:

Mark Yarnell, et al, *Self-Wealth*™
C/O Paper Chase Press
5721 Magazine St, Suite 152
New Orleans, LA 70115

Recommended Readings

The following are our favorite books that have helped us in our journey to Self-Wealth.

Albom, Mitch. *Tuesdays with Morrie - An Old Man, a Young Man and the Last Great Lesson*. New York: Bantum Doubleday, 1997.

Bandura, Albert, PH.D. *Self-Efficacy: The Exercise of Control*. New York: WH Freeman, 1997.

Benson, Herbert. *The Mind/Body Effect*. New York: Simon and Schuster, 1979.

Blanchard, Kenneth H. *The One Minute Manager*. Berkley: Berkley Publishing, 1983.

Butterworth, Eric. *Discover the Power Within You*. San Francisco: Harper Collins, 1992.

Cappon, Daniel, PH.D. *Intuition - Harnessing the Hidden Power of the Mind*. New York: Greenwood.

Carnegie, Dale. *How To Win Friends and Influence People*. New York: Simon & Schuster, 1982

Covey, Stephen R. *The Seven Habits of Highly Effective People*. New York, Simon & Schuster, 1990

Danforth, William H. *I Dare You.* I Dare You Committee.

Dyer, Wayne, PH.D. *Your Erroneous Zones*. New York: Harper Collins, 1993.

Hill, Napoleon. *Think and Grow Rich*. New York: Ballentine, 1937.

Houston, Jean, PH.D. *The Search for the Beloved: Journeys in Sacred Psychology*.

Houston, Jean, PH.D. *A Passion for the Possible: A Guide to Realizing Your True Potential*. New York: Harper Collins, 1997.

Keen, Sam, PH.D. *To Love and Be Loved*. New York: Bantam Books, 1997.

Mandela, Nelson. *Long Walk To Freedom: The Autobiography of Nelson Mandela*. New York: Little, Brown, and Co., 1995.

McDonald, John. *The Message of a Master*. Novato, Calif.: New World Library, 1993.

Peale, Norman Vincent. *If You Think You Can, You Can*. New York: Simon & Schuster, 1982.

Peale, Norman Vincent. *The Power of Positive Thinking*. New York: Simon & Schuster, 1987.

Parry, Danaan. *Warriors of the Heart: A Handbook for Conflict Resolution*. Baimbrige Island, Wash: Earth Stewards Network, 1997.

Pilkner, Steven. *How the Mind Works*. New York: Norton, 1999.

Ponder, Catherine. *The Dynamic Laws of Prosperity*. New York: DeVorss & Co., 1972.

Robins, Anthony. *Awaken the Giant Within*. New York: Simon & Schuster, 1991.

Robins, Anthony. *Unlimited Power*. New York: Simon & Schuster, 1986.

Rogers, Carl, PH.D. *A Way of Being*. New York: Houghlin Mifflin, 1995.

Siegal, Bernie, PH.D. *Perscriptions for Living: Inspirational Lessons for a Joyful, Loving Life*. New York: Harper Collins, 1999.

Waitley, Dennis, PH.D. *The Psychology of Winning*. Berkley, Calif.: Berkley Publishing Group, 1994.

Wheatley, Margaret, PH.D. *Leadership and the New Science*. New York: Berrett-Koehler, 1992.

Williams, A.L. *All You Can Do Is All You Can Do But All You Can Do is Enough*. New York: Random House, 1989.

INDEX

Self–Wealth™ Workshops

Our mission is to make a difference in people's lives. We offer a variety of workshops to help you in your journey to experiencing Self-Wealth in your life.

The Speakers

Mark Yarnell and his colleagues Valerie Bates and Dr. John Radford have made the Self-Wealth™ workshops exciting interactive events designed to help individuals address all areas of their lives for a richer, more rewarding life. Mark, Valerie and John are recognized world-wide for their speaking skills.

"I've heard hundreds of professional speakers. Mark Yarnell is quite literally a 'wordsmith,' and powerful speaker."
–Terry Townsend,
President Emeritus, National Society of Association Executives

The Training

Workshops vary in length from 1-day, 3 to 6 hour events, to 2-day weekend packages. Workshops can be customized to emphasize certain aspects for special groups, organizations, and corporate requirements. We offer pre-training assessment and recommendation, custom facilitation/training, and post-workshop evaluation.

FOR DATES AND TIMES OF WORKSHOPS IN YOUR AREA,
or for further information,

watch the Self-Wealth™ Newsletter,

check out our websites at:Self-Wealth.com or MarkYarnell.com,

or call: **1-800/460-8604.**

The Self-Wealth™ Newsletter!

FREE motivational/inspirational tape created by Mark Yarnell
with each issue!

5 issues/including 1 tape each issue
for $49.95/year; $99.95/3 years

The Self-Wealth™ Newsletter is a great place to change your life. This upbeat, informative, entertaining, inspirational newsletter can help you in your quest to achieve the most in life. Written by the most interesting and informed authors, speakers, researchers and thinkers on the cutting edge of self-improvement and life-changing technologies, this newsletter is an absolute must-have.

Order now for your FREE first issue,
or check out the newsletter on our website: Self-Wealth.com
For ordering information call: **1-800/460-8604**

Visit our website:

Self–Wealth.com

What can you find at Self-Wealth.com?

- Self-Wealth™ Newsletter

- Excerpts from Self-Wealth™, the book

- Special messages from Mark Yarnell, Valerie Bates, and Dr. John Radford

- engagements/public appearances for Mark Yarnell, Valerie Bates, and Dr. John Radford

- Self-Wealth™ workshop listings

- Product descriptions

- & much more

Mark Yarnell's Non-Profit Organizations

Mark Yarnell has always sought to make the world a better place. In his effort to create a goal bigger than himself, Mark has established several non-profit organizations. Anyone wishing to contribute to any or all of these organizations can call 1-800/460-8604 for information.

School of Sobriety

Mark struggled with alcohol and drugs for years. He decided to not only change his life in this area, but also to help others with the same struggle. In 1990, Mark founded the only free treatment School of Sobriety for alcoholics and addicts in Nevada.

"The Eagles:" Prison Reading/Self-Help Programs

For some time, Mark has had a special desire to help inmates at prisons learn to read and to develop personal skills to begin a new and better life. Mark funds reading and special personal development training programs in prisons in Nevada. Thousands have benefited from these programs, and despite his busy schedule, Mark continues to visit and teach at prisons.

"International Green Cross"

Mark is very concerned about the welfare of people and of our planet's ecosystem, and has been an instrumental source of funding for the International Green Cross.

A consummate outdoors person and nature lover, Mark is eager to reverse existing damage, and to preserve what we have. He is also gravely concerned about the proliferation of nuclear arms. He has joined Mikhail Gorbachev and Al Gore in a common mission to address these concerns.